LOCOMOTIVE PORTFOLIOS

P E P Prototype Trains, Classes 313, 314, 315, 507, 508

LOCOMOTIVE PORTFOLIOS

P E P Prototype Trains, Classes 313, 314, 315, 507, 508

GRAEME GLEAVES

PEN & SWORD TRANSPORT
AN IMPRINT OF PEN & SWORD BOOKS LTD.
YORKSHIRE – PHILADELPHIA

First published in Great Britain in 2026 by
Pen and Sword Transport
An imprint of
Pen & Sword Books Ltd.
Yorkshire – Philadelphia

Print ISBN 978 1 03610 247 0
ePUB ISBN 978 1 03610 248 7
ePDF ISBN 978 1 03610 250 0

A CIP catalogue record for this book is available from the British Library.

Typeset in Palatino by SJmagic DESIGN SERVICES, India.

Printed and bound in India by Replika Press Pvt. Ltd.

The Publisher's authorised representative in the EU for product safety is Authorised Rep Compliance Ltd., Ground Floor, 71 Lower Baggot Street, Dublin D02 P593, Ireland. www.arccompliance.com

For a complete list of Pen & Sword titles please contact

PEN & SWORD BOOKS LIMITED
George House, Beevor Street, Off Pontefract Road, Hoyle Mill, Barnsley, South Yorkshire, England, S71 1HN.
E-mail: enquiries@pen-and-sword.co.uk
Website: www.pen-and-sword.co.uk

or

PEN AND SWORD BOOKS
1950 Lawrence Rd, Havertown, PA 19083, USA
E-mail: uspen-and-sword@casematepublishers.com
Website: www.penandswordbooks.com

FSC
www.fsc.org
MIX
Paper | Supporting responsible forestry
FSC™ C016779

CONTENTS

Introduction 6

Chapter 1 The Ashes and the Phoenix 8

Chapter 2 The PEP 11

Chapter 3 PEP, Testing, Trials and Retirement 23

Chapter 4 The Class 313 39

Chapter 5 The Class 507 70

Chapter 6 The Class 314 78

Chapter 7 The Class 508 93

Chapter 8 The Class 315 119

Chapter 9 Epilogue 142

Appendix 1 The Preserved Units 143

Appendix 2 Vehicle Types and Numbers 154

Bibliography 156

Index 157

INTRODUCTION

The origins of this book date back to early 2021 when I was invited to take part in a discussion group to look at possible future acquisitions for the National Collection in the field of multiple units, which are now, of course, the most dominant form of rail passenger carrier. The meeting had been set up during the days of COVID so all delegates were to join remotely via their laptops and mobile devices. It was a gathering of the great and the good in the field of railway heritage and multiple unit preservation and their brief was to try to reach a consensus on what the important stories were regarding the newer generations of multiple unit, how they impacted both the industry and the people who worked and travelled on it, and then what would be the items needed for the National Collection to tell those stories. Given my experience in the field of electric multiple unit (EMU) preservation, I went into it with both an open mind as to what others felt was relevant but also with more than a few ideas of my own, which, given the space and financial limitations placed upon the National Collection, would have to be not only relevant but also streamlined and practically achievable whilst still meeting the brief.

The meeting went very well and there were a number of good ideas, all derived from some intelligent and experienced perspectives. Everyone knew that there were not the resourcse to save 'one of everything' but also that to do nothing would be a mistake that future generations would not thank us for. I had championed the idea that the 313 class of EMU was a really significant step change for British Rail and along with the High Speed Train, developed around the same time, represented the exact point in time when the industry in this country finally cast off the shackles of its troubled past and embraced the prospect of having a future based on the newest technology.

As the meeting went on, I became more convinced that this is what the National Collection should be doing, this was the story of that era as far as our passenger railways were concerned and I made great efforts to convey those thoughts to my fellow delegates. The meeting ended with me being tasked to write a paper on the points I had made: why was the class important; what stories did it tell; how could it be represented in the collection; and what were the challenges of making it happen.? This I duly did and the paper was presented a few weeks later; what happened next will be covered much later in this book but it dawned on me whilst writing that paper that this story would make a decent book; perhaps I could do that too?

Well, here it is, a while later and I didn't want to start work on it until the story that I wanted to tell had reached its notable conclusion. At the time of the meeting there were still nearly all classes of unit that made up the family in regular traffic, with the exception of the 314s. But, one by one over the next couple of years they all started to be replaced and I ventured out getting images of their last months (some of which are in this book) and following posts made online by enthusiasts who were documenting both the final workings and the withdrawals, along with the inevitable trips to the scrap yard for nearly all the units. There were of course the various attempts at preservation, some more credible than others and by the time I sat down to begin work on expanding that paper for the 313 into this book the story was told and I could cover it from beginning to end; well, the end for most of the units – but that will also be covered in detail later on.

When writing this I was reminded of the first time I became aware of the 313s. As I was born and raised in North Kent I had no idea such things existed due to our daily diet of slam door units that ran past the garden behind our family home. It was when I was on a trip to visit my grandparents in South London during 1977 and I was bought a packet of train themed 'Top Trumps', the card game that was a part of my childhood. Amongst the cards that all featured British diesel and electric locomotives was a selection of multiple units, one of which was the 313, which turned out to be a good card in the game as it was much longer than a locomotive (the highest number won in the game) and was also new (the most recent date also won). I remember being surprised that there were trains as new as this as the railway I knew didn't have anything that wasn't old and a bit tatty. That pack of Top Trumps was a great education to my 9-year-old self, for not only did it introduce me to the 313 it also taught me that the diesels that ran past my garden were called Class 33s and by looking at the photos I eventually worked out how the Total Operations Processing System (TOPS) numbers worked as the first two digits of a locomotive's number was its class and the same applied for multiple units, but it was the first three digits. I owe a lot to that game!

I must thank a number of people for their contributions and inspiration. Firstly Mike Lamport for his encouragement whilst part of the Railway Heritage Designation Advisory Board, Neil Bennett for giving me some insight into his experience in the world of rolling stock leasing, my fellow author Malcolm Batten, who, thanks to a chance meeting was able to furnish me with a bountiful supply of photos, many of which are in this volume. Also Colin Whitbread who once again came to the rescue with many pictures. Colin Marsden has been a great source of help and photographs, Colin was 'in the room when it happened' in the testing of the Prototype Electro Pneumatic Trains (PEP) and the introduction of the 508s and that knowledge was most useful. I'm grateful to Khai Slater, Robert Hampton and Shaun Henry for photos and information on their respective preservation projects. Thanks are also due to David Silman for allowing me to tap into his vast technical knowledge having been involved with 315 units for many years, John Scott-Morgan and the team at Pen and Sword for giving me the chance to get this work published, thank you for your patience! Also thanks are due to the other photographers who have given permission for their work to be included and they are credited where their work is used. I must also thank the guardians of the surviving units for their updates and help in sourcing pictures, please keep up the good work everyone. Finally, thank you to my wife Karen for putting up with me!

Graeme Gleaves
Croydon

The Top Trumps card for the 313, not my original one. This one belonged to a friend who had taken better care of his set than I had! Author

Chapter 1

THE ASHES AND THE PHOENIX

Back in the early 1970s the situation on Britain's rail network was certainly not shiny and new, in fact quite the opposite. British Rail, as it was now known was an industry that had been in sharp decline and was still shell shocked from the effects of the previous decade. To understand this we must go back to the last time our railways attempted be become modern.

Early in December 1954 the British Transport Commission published a plan simply called 'The Modernisation and Re-Equipment of the British Railways', it would eventually become known as the '1955 Modernisation Plan'. Within it was the announcement that the whole of the network would benefit from a huge investment in new locomotives, carriages and goods rolling stock along with new signalling and in some areas, electrification. Steam traction would be phased out and where new electric trains could not yet be provided then new classes of diesel locomotives and diesel railcars would be built to offer the passengers a more modern and efficient alternative to the worn out network they currently had.

All of this was highly ambitious and very expensive; even at the time it was costed at £1 billion and the money would be supplied to the industry by the treasury to be repaid by the expected increases in revenue the new look modern railway network could expect to collect from passengers and freight customers, along with the capital savings that the efficiency the modernisation would bring compared with its steam powered predecessor.

On paper it all made perfect sense, Britain's rail network was in a sorry state and most of that was down to the battering it took during the war years a decade earlier. Investment and modernisation were certainly the way to go. The government backed the plan with a White Paper that authorised the expenditure and even predicted British Railways could be profitable as early as 1962. In reality, things went very wrong in so many areas. A lot of the new forms of traction were ordered from multiple builders, some of whom had not done the correct amount of research and development and there were some notably poor designs that gave nothing but trouble. Additionally there were too many regional variations and efforts to standardise were lost. A good example of this was that the Western Region insisted on diesel-hydraulic transmission for its locomotives whilst the rest of the country opted for diesel-electric.

But by far the biggest mistake made was that the plan made no allowance for the social changes taking place in the country that were having a big impact on how people viewed and used the railways. Car ownership was on the rise due to the end of petrol rationing and the population aspired to own their own vehicles and enjoy the perceived freedoms that ownership offered them. Trains were a transport associated with years gone by and not what postwar Britons wanted. In addition, the handling of freight was moving away from individual wagon loads and small loads, which were also moving to road haulage and it was only the large bulk traffic that was continuing to remain loyal to rail. It wasn't too long before all of this began to bite and it became clear that the cost of the Modernisation Plan was never going to be repaid. It would be unfair to say that every aspect of the plan was a failure, that would be patently untrue; the electrification schemes in Kent, Glasgow and the West Coast Main Line between London and Liverpool and Manchester had delivered a vastly improved service and resulted in rail continuing to keep its traffic. Not all the locomotives and railcars were troubled, many classes were built that would go on to give decades of good service. However, it was the branch lines and secondary routes that were suffering badly and the costs of running these far outstripped the revenue they generated. The railways had needed modernisation, of that there was no doubt, but they also needed to be re-defined to meet the needs of the world they now served. As they had failed to do that, and by 1961 were losing money in the region of £300 000 per day, the prime minister, Harold Macmillan, who had told the population in a 1957 speech that they had 'never had it so good' was about to deliver quite the opposite message to British Railways.

The appointment of Dr Richard Beeching as Chairman of the British Railways Board in March 1961 was the start of what many consider to be the most seismic period in the history of the railway industry in Britain. He had been put into the position with one job, to make the railways pay their way. To achieve this he commissioned a survey be undertaken of the levels of traffic on all lines in an effort to find out what was profitable and what wasn't. In March 1963, two years after he took up his position, his report was published. Entitled 'The Reshaping of British Railways' the report proposed the closure of 6,000 miles of railways, including 2,363 stations; this accounted for about a third of the existing network. His report highlighted that the network suffered from a duplication of routes and that some of the least used lines were generating revenue that covered barely 10 per cent of their annual operating costs. Many of the arguments put forward were difficult to counter but over the next couple of years there was a lot of debate and protests, but mostly closures. A change of government from Harold Macmillan's Conservatives to Harold Wilson's Labour did little to halt the reduction in route miles, indeed some lines that had previously been omitted for closure in Beeching's original report were added to the closure list under the new government, mainly for political reasons as the routes listed for closure were in marginal constituencies and it was this, and not their commercial or social considerations that earned them a reprieve. One thing the period did prove was that no matter what government was in power, there was no way the railway industry would be allowed to write cheques it could not cash. From the perceived disaster of the 1955 Modernisation Plan, the industry was now on a very tight financial leash, presiding over a network that was at two thirds of its previous size and relying on hand outs to keep running. British Railways ran its last timetabled steam trains in August 1968, so one of the aims of the plan had finally been achieved. At the same time, locomotives and railcars that were either non-standard, unreliable or for which there was no longer any work were being disposed of. Many were less than a decade old and over the next few years many more would suffer a similar fate. Britain had given the railways to the world but now the country had virtually turned its back on them. The end of the 1960s were when, on the face of it, the industry must have considered itself at its lowest point ever.

Lessons were going to be learned and a few undeniable truths were exposed. Even Beeching had pointed out that there was a place for rail in Britain's future and the industry had to recognise quite where that future was, where the traffic that could 'pay its way' existed and if there was a revenue shortfall then how could it be made up? Beeching's report had highlighted the essential nature of commuter traffic in London and many other municipal cities and had suggested that 'It may well be up to the municipal authorities to work with both the rail and bus industries to produce a 'co-ordinated system of services'. Indeed, Beeching pointed out that it was unfair to expect locally subsidised bus services to compete with rail services that had no such subsidy and were expected to pay their own way.

In 1968, the government passed the Transport Act which enabled the creation of regional Passenger Transport Executives (or Authorities) which had the power to do just this, creating a joined up local transport policy between bus and rail. Perhaps as far as commuter traffic was concerned the 1970s would not be as bad for rail as the 1960s. It needs to be remembered that whilst lines and stations were being shut, Britain's railways were still looking to the future in many other areas; the West Coast Main line electrification was completed in the mid-1960s between Liverpool, Manchester, Birmingham and London and there were strong calls for the scheme to extend the length of the line to Glasgow. This was authorised in 1970, passenger numbers were rising on the route and this was to become one of the greatest success stories of the 1955 Modernisation Plan.

Elsewhere, railway research was being focused on a new headquarters in Derby, the Railway Technical Centre, which opened in May 1964 and would bring together previously separate research units involved in electrical, permanent way, rolling stock and other sciences used in the development of railways. This facility boasted state of the art test houses, workshops and laboratories. The intention was to have the means to design the rolling stock, motive power and infrastructure for the modern railway. All of this took place whilst the last few years of the steam age drew to a close in the North-West of England.

Another big development took place on 1 January 1970 when British Railways concentrated all of its in house heavy repair and railway vehicle construction sites under a new company called British Rail Engineering Limited (BREL). This comprised the major railway works that it had inherited from the big four in 1948, many of which went back over a century and included the locomotive and carriage works at Derby, the locomotive works at Crewe and Doncaster and the sites at Shildon, Eastleigh, Ashford, Glasgow, Swindon, Wolverton and York. The portfolio meant that every activity from construction to repair or overhaul of anything from a locomotive, carriage or wagon, down to individual components could be undertaken in house and over time sites were re-organised to specialise in one or two aspects of the process rather than trying to spread themselves too thinly. The intention was for BREL to not only supply the domestic rail industry but to be an exporter of equipment to the world.

The network had itself been rebranded to go forward. As previously mentioned railways were considered a thing of the past in some quarters so a new image was created for British Railways. The name was shortened to British Rail in 1965 and a simple, but instantly recognisable new logo with two rail lines and a pair of opposing arrows across them was designed as the brand identity. The colour scheme of the new organisation would also change, with green locos becoming all over blue and the coaching stock becoming blue with grey around the windows. Sub brands such as Inter-City for the express services from London to Scotland, South Wales, the West Country and eastern counties was launched and the new corporate identity began to be applied across the network in an effort to stamp out the memory of the bad old days and promote an industry that was intent on looking to a future. What it needed now were trains that were equally forward thinking to run the services.

Some would say that the changes forced upon the industry in the wake of the Beeching era were the changes it should have made itself in the 1950s with a bringing together of its many facilities and departments and concentrating on the services that the country needed rather than those it felt obligated to provide at whatever cost. The railway that went into the 1970s was leaner and better organised but were these changes going to be enough? The industry would never again see the capital from the treasury it had once relied upon handed over without being able to justify the costs with hard facts and a decent business plan. This was now the way the railways were going to be modernised or face further decline.

Chapter 2

THE PEP

In 1960s Britain there were two schools of thought when it came to the design of new EMUs. Firstly, there were those built by British Railway workshops who had perpetuated a policy primarily inherited from the Southern Railway, whereby electric units were simply motorised versions of the regular coaches used on the network with minimal variation where necessary. In the case of British Railways this meant that their units were based on the standard Mark I coach, the express version had gangways, a mix of compartments with side corridor or open plan setting in bays of four arranged around the layout of the bodyside windows. At the ends and middle of the coach would be the single leaf doors that were hinged and slammed shut, opened and closed by the passengers themselves.

The suburban version followed the pattern of the suburban Mark I coach in that is was non-gangwayed and had either closed compartments the width of the coach or semi-saloons which were half the length of the coach with 3 + 2 seating in bays. Some units had first class where traffic demanded it and this was always in compartments with side corridors. The suburban coaches had a door to every seating bay on the carriage and these were also hinged 'slam doors' opened and closed by the passengers. The suburban coach was termed 'high density' as it had far more seats than its express counterpart as commuter traffic was, for a couple of hours in the morning and evening, dealing with very heavy demand. Anyone who experienced suburban commuting during the decades of operation of stock of this type will easily be able to recount similar stories of why it was such an unpleasant experience. The trains had been designed to offer as many people as possible a seat but during the busiest period there was no hope of this and only the lucky ones who boarded the train furthest from its destination would get to sit down. The closer it got to the city the more people joined and this highlighted one of the shortcomings of the suburban stock design, there was no allocated standing space for them, except in the aisles, between the seating bays, on the toes of those who were sitting down, between the seats in the full width compartments or even in the guard's luggage space if you were permitted entry. The design did not lend itself to the crush loading that was regularly experienced during the height of the morning and evening peaks. The presence of so many doors on a suburban train were certainly efficient at loading and unloading passengers in the bustle of the rush hours but they came with the risk that doors that weren't closed properly had to be checked by the station staff of the guard on the train, causing delay and at very busy stations there was no way of stopping late comers from attempting to board a train even if it was moving, which resulted in occasional injuries and many more delays.

The other school of EMU building was that applied by the London Underground. They, like many of the London bound BR commuter routes, had exceptionally high traffic numbers during the morning and evening peaks but the nature of their operation meant that they had extra tools at their disposal to help tackle this. The dedicated routes meant they didn't have to share with express or freight traffic, so a far more intensive timetable could be run with a standard 'all stations' calling pattern, with the exception of the Metropolitan Line of course. Their trains ran in tunnels for much of their distance so from the very beginnings they never had slam doors, except on the sub surface lines.

By the start of the early part of the twentieth century, even those lines would change to hand operated sliding doors (except the longer distance Metropolitan services). All of this shaped their future EMU designs and by the 1930s the new standard stock had air doors in wide pairs with three sets per coach side, seating in both bays and longitudinal benches, but plenty of standing room around the door pockets for crush loading as well as leather handles for those standing in the central aisles to hold onto when they couldn't get a seat, giving rise to the term 'strap hangers'. The air doors were by then all under the control of the train crew who dictated when they were open and closed; of course, there was still the potential for people to hold the doors open with feet and hands to allow a late running fellow passenger to board but otherwise when a pair of doors was shut it stayed shut and late comers were going to have to wait for the next train. London Underground knew they were never going to be able offer everyone a seat so accepted standing as part of the everyday operations of the network and provided space for it to be done. Of course one significant difference between the Underground and British Railways was that the former did not build their own trains but contracted the construction out to private builders, including British Railways' own workshops, who built the trains to the specifications issued by London Transport. It is also important to note that EMU fleets built for British Railways' routes by private builders followed London Underground practice, which is why parts of Liverpool, Manchester, Glasgow and the East of London and Essex suburban routes had units with air doors and standing space long before the Southern Region even considered it.

Commuter traffic was both the highest earning and most secure sector of the railway's passenger business, so money could be requested and possibly authorised by the Treasury for its upkeep and renewal when that request was supported with a robust business case. During the late 1960s, thoughts turned to the replacement of ageing units operating in the areas of South and East London along with Liverpool, where many of the then current fleets were of pre-war vintage. In addition, there were ambitions to push through new schemes for the electrification of heavily used but currently ill equipped suburban routes and the provision of new stock for those operations. Unlike the rush to push something into service that had been a folly of the 1955 Modernisation Plan, British Rail decided to call upon its newly organised team of designers, builders, research and development resources and come up with a standard concept that would form the basis of the next generation of commuter EMUs. The inspiration for these would not be the former British Railways/Southern template of slam doors and as many seats as possible, but the philosophy that had been applied to the London Underground. With new electrification schemes in Glasgow and the North of London authorised, there was now a ticking clock to have the new stock ready in time, approximately by late 1975, with replacement programmes for stock running on existing electrified lines to run until the beginning of the 1980s. A full scale wooden mock-up of a driving car, showing the outline and intended styling of the new stock, had been constructed at the Railway Technical Centre along with much smaller scale models to show the extent of the proposals. This forward planning gave a window of opportunity for BREL to build prototype sets based on the concepts that had been created for the vision of the requirements and the test them extensively before committing to the production build scheme.

The order was placed in 1970 and BREL set about the construction of three EMUs at their York works in Holgate Street, a location that had a history of building EMUs since the early 1900s. These were required to be passenger carrying prototypes that could be tested in service on a real timetable under 'live fire' conditions. To this end the three units were built as two 4-car sets and one 2-car set and they were constructed to operate on the third rail system of the Southern Region where they could be used on existing commuter traffic but also have access to the wider network to visit works and depots for maintenance, modifications and inspections. The three units all followed the same outline and had vehicles made of a mix of aluminium, steel and alloys with a combined bodyshell and underframe so the vehicles had no sole bar. The bogies and underfloor equipment were joined to the underside of the bodyshell which followed an outline that

differed from previous builds by BREL in that that had a pronounced outward curve at its lower third then a straight side that slanted up toward the roof line and then curved over the top of the body to form a flat roof. The ends of the body had a slight taper from the final few inches toward the central section which housed the gangways between vehicles on the non-driving ends but on the driving cabs the lines were different due to the need to provide cab windows on both sides of the cab front. The lower portion of the cab front tapered out and then raked back so the portion with the cab windows was at a slight back angle to give a subtle air of aerodynamics but this was somewhat ruined by the large cutout area between the cab windows where the front escape door was fitted, there being no connecting gangways on the front but the door was required to provide a means of evacuating the train in a tunnel or other place with restricted side clearance.

At the same height as the cab windows and set into the central door was a two digit roller blind head code box, the most traditional thing about these sets. Below the cab fronts was a major change to earlier generations of stock as these units had no buffers, instead the buffing forces were absorbed by the couplers which were of a new design for a train in Britain. Named 'Schaku' and manufactured by Scharfenberg, these were automatic couplings, which meant that the physical acts of locking them together (coupling) and unlocking them (uncoupling) were not undertaken by human labour but by operating controls in the cab. British Rail had shopped around various European manufacturers to find an automatic coupling it could adopt for its new rolling stock that would reduce the need for staff to go track side during coupling and uncoupling operations. Scharfenberg had a proven track record and were willing to supply a version of their coupling that could suit British Rail's requirements. Each coupling had a head with a male and female component that when brought together fitted into each other and a locking mechanism engaged. On each side of the coupler heads were electrical connections comprised of 36 brass studs that had a sliding cover, this cover automatically retracted when the coupler heads came together, exposing the brass studs which pushed against the corresponding exposed studs on the coupler it was connecting to to create a through electrical connection between the two units. The final part of the coupler was the two small air valves in the upper and lower centre which when coupled was formed into an airtight seal allowing compressed air to flow between the units. The lower edge of the coupler featured an angled metal bar that was set up to ensure the couplers met at the correct alignment and was known as the guide horn. The Scharfenberg arrangement meant that all the driver had to do when the two units

The wooden mock up of the proposed new high density suburban stock pictured outside the Railway Technical Centre in Derby. British Rail

coupled up was to press a button in the cab to confirm the correct coupling and this would electrically open the valves and relays to switch on the air and electrical connections between the units and tell the train's on board system that it was coupled in multiple. To uncouple it was just the reverse of this, press a button to cut off the air and electrical supplies and unlock the physical locking mechanism and then reverse the unit off the one it was to be uncoupled from. There was no need for a shunter to go in between the units and do any physical work as that was purpose of the automatic nature of the coupling. Of course automatic couplings had been in use on the London Underground since the late 1930s and now British Rail was playing catch up. These couplings were only fitted to the driving ends as it was decided that the individual cars of the units would only need to be separated for maintenance purposes so at the non-driving end a bar coupling was provided that had locator studs to maintain the alignment at its facing edges and four bolts around the head that were tensioned to hold the arrangement together. These were not new; this type of coupling had been developed in the 1960s for coupling semi-permanent rakes of freightliner flat wagons together. The bar went into a drag box under the body end where the buffing and draw forces were absorbed and transferred to the vehicle frame.

For a new generation of train the innovations didn't end with the couplings. These units were packed with new, or in the very least, 're-hashed' features. The passenger and crew doors were one of the latter. Where slam doors had held sway on BR built stock since nationalisation, air operated doors were now the preferred choice, again playing catch up with other builders of the last four decades. On driving cars, the passengers had two pairs of doors per side with a third door fitted behind the driving cab on each side for train crew use. The non-driving cars had three pairs of air operated doors per side. The operation of the doors as originally designed was that the doors would be electrically released by the guard of the train and passengers would open the ones they wanted to use by push buttons mounted adjacent to each set of doors. When it was time to depart and passengers were clear, the guard could press a button on their control panel and all doors would shut. A light would illuminate on the guard's panel to indicate that all doors had closed correctly and were secured shut. In practice during the testing there were issues with the door buttons and a modification was made to the units to remove them and replace with a system of passenger-initiated door opening. With the doors released by the guard, passengers now gripped a vertical bar fitted to the inside and outside of each door and started to pull the door open, once the door mechanism detected this slight movement air pressure took over and the door continued to open itself fully; the system worked the same in reverse if a passenger wanted to close a door. The closing of all doors on the train prior to departure remained with the guard as before. Inside, the trains had open saloons with seating in the areas between the door pockets in 2+2 layout, the bulk of which was uni-directional airline style but a bay of facing seats was provided in the centre of each cluster. The seats themselves were formed from moulded plastic bases with base and seat back cushions fitted to them, these could be removed for cleaning purposes. The backs were only half height, like on a bus, and this was because the thinking was that passenger journeys on the suburban metro were mostly short in duration and thus a higher level of comfort was not required. It should be noted that a higher backed seat design was trialled in two coaches of one set later in the test programme. The lower density provision of the seating and the empty spaces where the door pockets were allowed for plenty of standing room for rush hour traffic and it was estimated that more passengers could be accommodated in a coach standing than there was provision for seated ones. The design did not provide any grab handles for standing passengers to steady themselves on other than the upright aluminium poles on the end of each draught screen that shielded the seating areas from the door pockets. Seating capacity of the driving cars was 68 and 72 in the non-driving cars. The area surrounding the driving cab was best described as a 'lobby' with an open space containing some of the on train emergency equipment. Between the single leaf door and the left hand cab front was the driving position which was mounted in a cupboard type assembly between the left hand side of the central escape door and the cab end leaf door. Guards also used this area as no brake van was provided specifically for them. Heating and ventilation used a system of vents in the roof with a heating and ventilation module provided in each coach. Two motors in this module would either draw air in from atmosphere where it was passed over a heating element if probes within the coach itself detected sufficiently low temperature. From here it was sent down ducting into the coach interior. If the temperature was high enough to require the interior to be cooled, then the heating motors would automatically be switched to run in reverse, thereby drawing air down the ducting from the interior, the thinking being that cooler air from the atmosphere through vents in the roof would be drawn into the interior and keep the coach cool. In reality it was found that this system was not sufficient to prevent the saloons from become 'stuffy' on hot days and this prompted a modification of all the large bodyside windows that been delivered as sealed double glazed units. The modification consisted of replacing these with units that had a sliding section of window in the upper quarter and this was completed before the units carried their first passengers. The interior lighting was provided by fluorescent tubes which worked from an AC supply from the unit's motor alternator set. Because these could not be fed from the train's battery supply, in the event of third rail power being lost there were incandescent lamps fitted in the

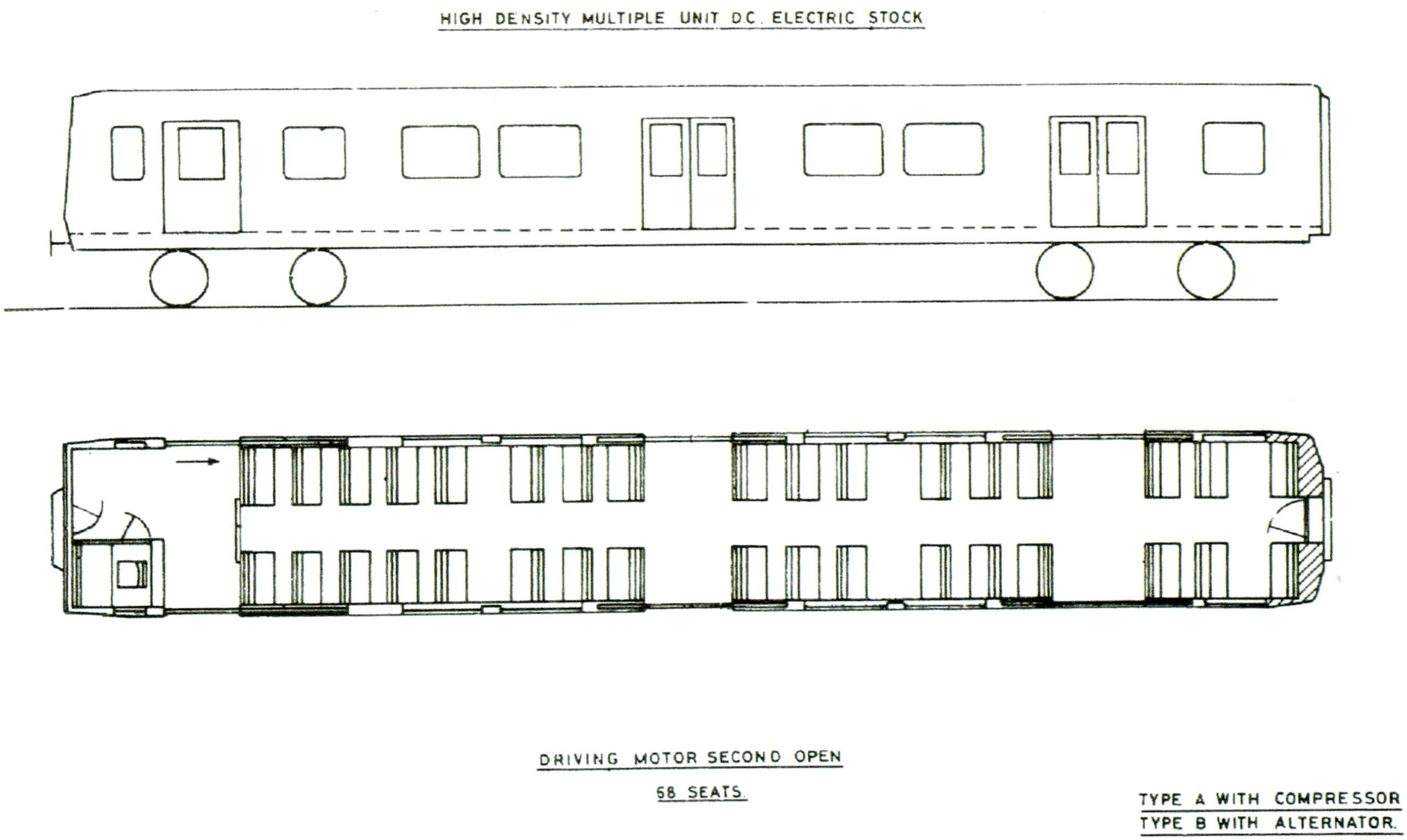

Diagram of the side elevation and interior layout of a driving motor second car. British Rail

ceiling of each door pocket that were fed from 110V DC, obtained from either the motor alternator or the batteries, as was all the lighting in the cab and on the front of the train. This supply also fed the control circuits on the unit.

As futuristic as this train looked above platform level there was even more innovation underneath the body. The biggest departure from previous norms was that every axle of the train had its own 100hp traction motor. Previously traction motors have been provided on a ratio of roughly 25 per cent of the axles of a 2- to 4-car set, the thinking being that more motors would enable smoother and swifter acceleration and distribute the weight evenly along the length of the train to even out track wear and rolling resistance. The motors on each bogie were connected in permanent series with both series and parallel configuration possible between each bogie. Control of traction voltage was by means of camshaft control, whereby an oil operated motor switched resistance in and out of circuit as road speed increases to allow for controlled acceleration; this method of motor control had been in widespread use in the UK since the mid-1930s so there was nothing new in that respect, but the distribution of motors was a real first. Each coach had its own camshaft and resistances and it was envisaged that on

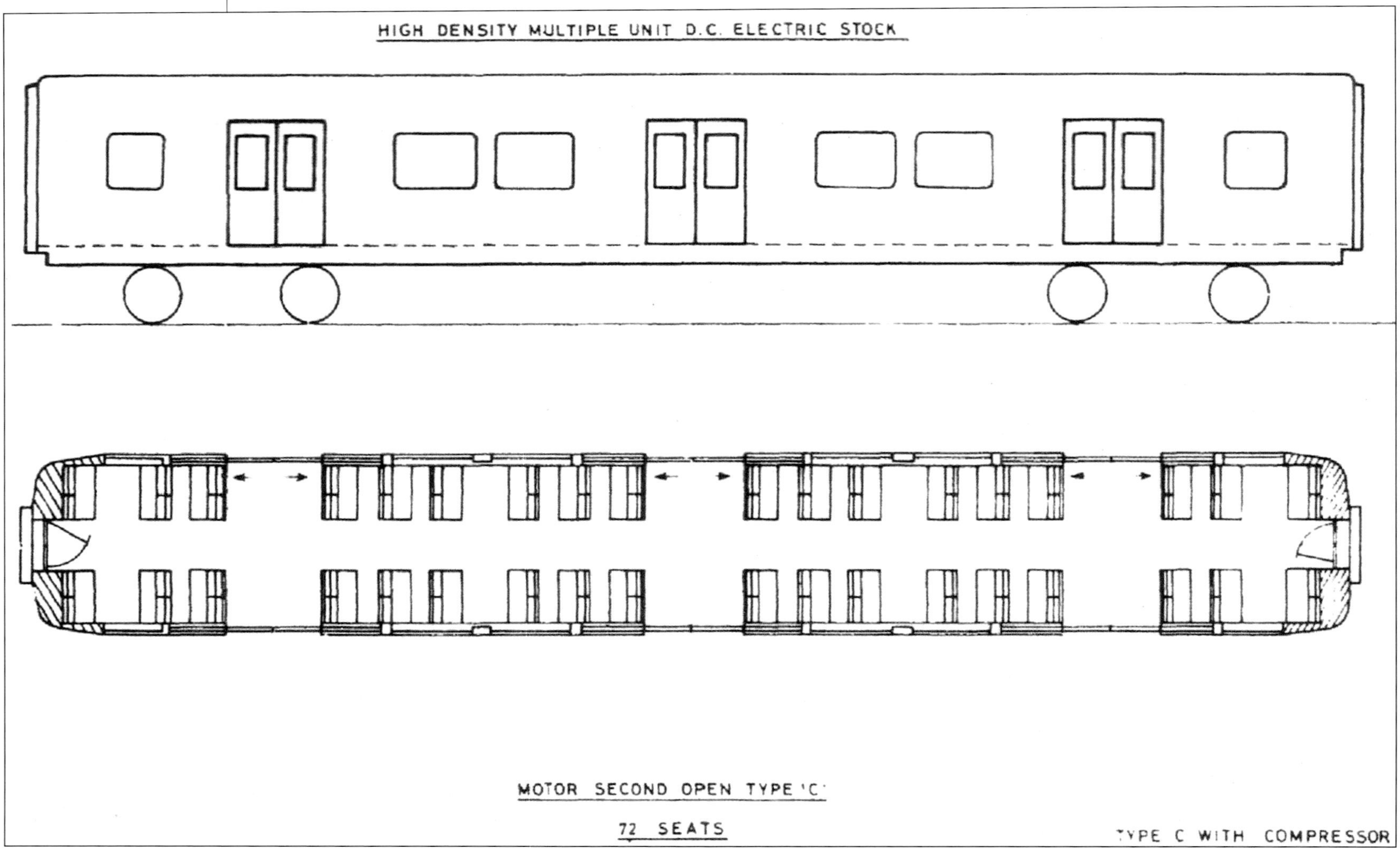

Diagram of the side elevation and interior layout of a non'driving motor second car. British Rail

level track the train would draw 330 amps per motor upon starting and give an acceleration rate of 2mph per second. Self protection relays were fitted to detect wheel slip during acceleration. This was something the Railway Technical Centre had researched and had been a developing feature for locomotives and EMUs over the last decade so the PEP got the latest version. It was also provided with overload protection on each coach to prevent excessive current reaching the motors.

In addition to the motors and their associated control equipment there was also equipment mounted under each coach in order to distribute the weight. This varied from coach to coach. In the case of a 4-car unit it needed two compressors and two motor alternators; the former created compressed air for the brakes and suspension and the later produced the 240V AC and 110V DC previously mentioned for lighting and battery charging. For the purposes of equipment layout and distribution it was best to think of a 4-car unit as two 2-car sets back to back. Each half consisted of a 'B Coach' which was a driving end with a motor alternator and battery set mounted underneath. Adjacent to it was a 'C Coach' which was a non-driving coach with a compressor mounted underneath. There was a 750V bus line between the B and C coaches but not between the point in the middle of the train where the two C coaches were coupled together. Collector shoes for the third rail were mounted either side on the cab end bogie of each driving car and the inner bogie of each non-driving car. In the case of the 2-car set, which had no non-driving car, there was a need to have an 'A Coach'. This was a driving car that did not have a motor alternator or batteries but did have a compressor, so if you think of an A Coach as a B Coach from platform

The layout of the jumpers and car types in a six car PEP formation taken from the official driver's manual. British Rail

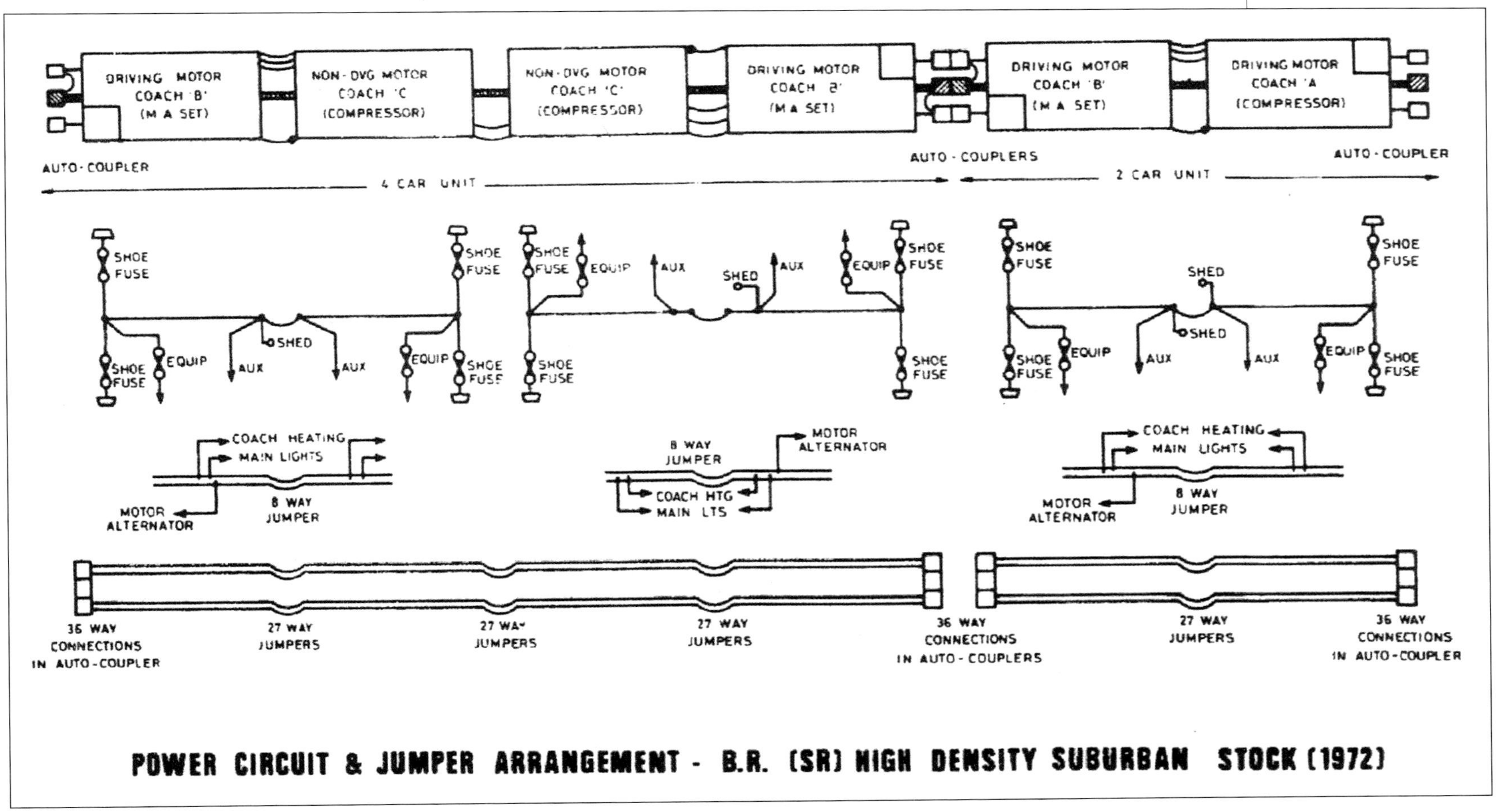

level up and a C Coach from below platform level then you have it. The diagram on the previous page should enable this all to make sense.

Suspension was a two part affair with the primary being the coil springs mounted either side of the axle boxes. Secondary suspension was a new air-based system that could be inflated or deflated subject to loading demands. A loading valve incorporated into the air suspension detected when a vehicle was getting heavier when more people got on board and it was this valve that allowed more compressed air to enter the suspension bags on that coach which were mounted on the bolsters of the bogies. As people started to leave the vehicle later in the journey, this reduction in weight was also detected and compressed air was released from the suspension bags to return them to their nominal operating pressure. Each coach had its own air tank for compressed air to feed the air suspension which acted as a header tank to smaller surge tanks which meant that movements in the suspension caused by the motion of the train in traffic could be compensated for without draining the main suspension tank before it could be replenished. Given that every axle was motored there was only a requirement to fit one type of bogie to the train and during the life of the PEP units various modifications and alternative bogie types were trialled.

It was perhaps the braking system that was the boldest change from anything seen before on British Railways. The motorisation of every axle opened up the possibility of using rheostatic braking. This system utilised the traction resistances and camshaft to use the energy generated by the traction motors when coasting (a motor behaves like a dynamo when not under power). The energy the motor creates is fed back into the traction resistances and it is this resistance that forces the motor to slow down. This process creates a lot of heat and fans were provided under each coach, fed from the motor alternator supply, that force cooled the traction resistances during rheostatic braking. Rheostatic braking had limitations. Firstly it was not failsafe; this was a requirement for passenger trains in Britain so the rheostatic could not be used as the only brake on the train. Secondly, rheostatic braking became less efficient the lower the rail speed of the train. To overcome both of these issues the train was fitted with a Westcode electro-pneumatic friction brake. This was a system whereby air from the train's main reservoirs could be injected into the brake cylinders by the operation of electrical control wires along the length of the train. This could be achieved by use of the driver's brake control handle which when moved energised combinations of control wires to instruct the train how much air to inject. As each coach had its own Westcode brake control unit and they were all linked together by a control line, the driver's actions applied or released the brakes equally on all cars simultaneously. The Westcode system was failsafe as it relied on one control wire to be energised at all times. If it was broken anywhere in the train by the operation of a passenger alarm, an emergency brake application by the guard or the train accidentally dividing that wire would fail and the train's brakes would become fully applied. It also functioned better at low speeds than the rheostatic, but the rheostatic was far better at higher speeds so it was arranged that the train would employ rheostatic braking from maximum design speed down to 13mph, after which the Westcode system would automatically take over and slow the train to a stop if required. The Westcode system was capable of operating over seven different steps but to keep the system simple from the outset it only employed three and the driver's brake controller in the cab was marked as such and only had three braking positions other than the release one. An emergency position was also provided and this would operate even in cabs that were not live, giving the guard access to an emergency brake to stop the train if necessary. The controller controlled both the rheostatic and Westcode systems, depending which the train was using at that time. During colder weather, provision was made to divert some of the heat created by rheostatic braking into the train's heating system. One final thing that needs mentioning was the provision of the hydraulic parking brakes. Since time began on the railway, the hand brake on any vehicle had been a manual affair that used either a lever or a winding mechanism operated by the train crew to physically apply the brake blocks against the running surface of the wheels on any vehicle that was to be parked for any period of time. The PEP did away with this with a parking brake that was applied by operation of switches in the cab. It was not the first time something like this had seen use on the Southern Region as the first batch of CIG units had employed a rudimentary electric parking brake but this was an enhanced version of that system that was back for another chance to be proved in service. There were a few other features of the unit that would have been familiar to train crew in addition to the two character roller headcode blinds; the cab to cab communication was of the Loudaphone type that had been a feature of Southern units for over ten years and the driving controller, reversing switch and indicator flags from the desk that showed the status of various equipment were identical to those used on the VEP and CIG units.

Photos of the cab interior showing the basic layout and the features such as the loudaphone and master controller that were carried over from previous builds. British Rail

The PEPs, being suburban units, were built with a maximum design speed of 75mph and work continued on them during 1970 until the late spring of 1971 when the first of the 4-car units was ready to deliver to the Southern Region so it could commence testing.

In the autumn of 1971 the first PEP set No. 4001 was frequently seen under the great roof at Waterloo performing test operations over many different routes. On 9 September 1971, the set is seen in platform 15 at Waterloo with a test run back to Waterloo via Hounslow and Twickenham '89' this was before the window modification took place. Colin Marsden

Unit 2001 leads a six car PEP formation on a Waterloo to Hampton Court service past Wimbledon West Yard.
Colin Marsden

***Below left*: The interior** of a driving car, looking inward from the first set of passenger doors. Note the low back seats with grab handles at the top, aluminium luggage racks and hidden florescent lighting. Wall panels were a style of Formica. Taken before the opening windows were installed.
Colin Marsden

***Below right*: 4001 at** York Works 19 May 1971 during static testing.
Colin Marsden

Construction of the 10 PEP vehicles was undertaken by BREL York Works from summer 1970. Just prior to delivery to Wimbledon for testing No. 4001 is seen inside York Works on 19 May 1971. Of interest is that the unit numbers are under the black paint on the front which could indicate the black window surrounds were a late addition.
Colin Marsden

In as-delivered condition, without sliding top light windows, set No. 4001 is seen between Alton and Farnham in summer 1972. The set carried standard rail blue livery with yellow/black cab ends and deep brown underframe and bogies. Note the power pick ups are at set ends and the inner end of the attached intermediate coach. Colin Marsden

Chapter 3

PEP, TESTING, TRIALS AND RETIREMENT

The first unit, numbered 4001, was hauled from York to Temple Mills in the first week of July 1971. After a brief stopover at Stratford it was then hauled direct to Wimbledon Park depot where it arrived on 7 July. As these units were unique, they would only couple to each other so the movement of them required the conversion of 'match wagons' to translate the Schaku couplers of the driving ends to conventional buffers and draw hooks as used by BR locomotives. The buffers were removed from one end of the selected wagons and replaced with the Schaku coupling gear, including a drag box that would handle all the buffing and draw forces. The other ends of the wagons were left as built and it was these ends the locomotive coupled to, with the unit coupled to the other; a second wagon had to be provided at the other end of the train as there was a requirement for the train locomotive to run around its load if it needed to reverse direction. There was also a requirement to be able to couple an assisting locomotive to the rear of a train that had broken down so it could be pushed or pulled clear of the running lines.

The movements posed another problem in that the brakes on the new EMU were not compatible with the brakes on the wagons or locomotives and the only way around this was to run the movements as an old style unfitted goods train, running at a reduced speed and relying purely on the locomotive brake and the manually operated handbrake in the guard's goods brake van at the rear of the train to stop the train at signals or in the event of an emergency. These limitations would stay with movement of PEP units not under their own power for the rest of their operating lives right up until they were towed away for disposal and carried on when the production units would be delivered.

As the units were heading to the Southern Region, the management of that division needed to create a three letter code to identify them, as they had done for all their fleet of EMUs. This is where the name PEP came from, but it was not the first choice. Originally the units were to become PER which stood for Prototype Electro Rheostatic, a designation that made reference to both their status as prototypes for evaluation and their groundbreaking (for the Southern Region) use of the rheostatic brake. Very late in the process this got changed to PEP (for reasons unknown), PEP stood for Prototype Electro Pneumatic. It must be stressed that the three prototype units, the two 4-cars and the 2-car were the only units ever to receive the designation of PEP, none of the classes built from the evaluation of those three units ever got that designation and when they are described as PEPs it is only a nickname and not an official designation; the three letter code was purely a Southern Region system and the production units were not built for that region. The TOPS system was by then also in use and the units needed a classification under which they could be recorded in the TOPS computer. Initially all three were to be class 461 but this was changed to class 445 for the 4-car units and class 446 for the single 2-car example. A curiosity about the numbering of the two 4-car units was that they used the same unit numbers, 4001 and 4002, as the last two prototype units that had been built for the Southern Region. They were the two 4-car double deck units that had emerged in 1949 and remained in use until 1971. The design was an attempt to squeeze more passengers into a standard length carriage by having offset compartments at two levels; the design was not a success and did not lead to any further units being built. Whether the re-use of those numbers was a coincidence or intended the spirit of the 4-DD was perpetuated in some small way in the 4-PEP is not known.

4001 arrived at Wimbledon Park painted in the BR corporate shade of blue with black/brown underfloor detail and bogies. The cab fronts were all yellow except the area around the front windows which was picked out in black. At the time this scheme was still quite new and had yet to be fully rolled out across all fleets it was important that the train of the future embraced the latest livery of the BR corporate era. 4001 was inspected by technicians and trainers for the next few weeks as they all tried to get to grips with the latest train on the network. Static testing was carried out inside the shed using the 750V DC shed supply. Eventually the unit would be allowed to move around within the depot limits and at some point it was cleared to go onto the main line. Unfortunately, history does not record the date of the first main line run of the PEP unit, or even where it went but what we do know is that by 13 September it was able to travel to Selhurst Depot and from there it went to Charing Cross on the following day where a press launch was held and journalists were able to look over this new product with senior managers on hand to explain the many benefits it would herald for the suburban railway commuter in the coming years. That done, the unit returned to Wimbledon to begin a rigorous programme of testing.

The testing focused on many areas, the first of which was that the unit would fit on the railway it was built for and could use the stations safely. This involved it being run through the stations on the routes it was to operate on and make simulated stops. The clearance between the train and the platform would be measured to ensure it complied with the requirements for stepping distances and that the body profile didn't

4001 (with unpainted driving car) trails 4002 on an 8-car service probably bound for Hampton Court, This photo was taken out of a train window near Raynes Park. 13.6.1976. Malcolm Batten

4002 Stewart's Lane. 22 June 1976, it had probably been moved here from Wimbledon Park in preparation for transit on to the RTC at Derby. Colin Whitbread

foul any of the structures on the station. The same had to be done for bridges and tunnels and also that the train could pass another train on an adjacent line travelling at line speed and there would be a sufficient clearance distance. It was also a requirement that the unit rode without any excessive pitch or sway when at speed from its suspension causing the body profile to shift out of gauge. Many of these runs were conducted at night when the railway wasn't as busy and the engineers could take their time ensuring they got the measurements right. Other testing focussed on the train's performance inasmuch as it could accelerate without drawing excessive current from the third rail and that it could slow itself down and also stop inside the required distances provided for by the signalling system. One area where high speed testing was carried out was the line between Aldershot and Alton, which had double track but a lot of spare capacity and would allow for the units to be tested up to their design maximum speed of 75mph. The units were also able to conduct these test runs during the day having run down from Wimbledon Park depot in the morning and held in the sidings at Aldershot between runs to allow service trains to pass.

4001 was joined by 4002, the second 4-car unit, at Wimbledon park depot on 11 November 1971. It had travelled the same route as 4001 but the pathing from Stratford to Wimbledon took a week to organise. 4002 was painted in the identical livery to 4001 and the only difference between them was the numbering. 4002 was quickly checked over and static tested

Interior of 4002 Stewart's Lane taken on 22 June 1976. Colin Whitbread

before it was given the all-clear to join 4001 on the testing programme. This also gave the engineers their first opportunity to couple the units up and see how they behaved when run as an 8-car formation; again, history didn't record the first time this happened.

The 2-car unit was going to be numbered 2001 and it would not be delivered straight from York to Wimbledon, going instead to the Railway Technical Centre at Derby for testing by the engineers there, but it wouldn't emerge from York for a few months but when it did it showed just how willing BR were to draw upon the experience of London Underground in designing EMUs. 2-car unit 2001 appeared in the late spring of 1972 and it was not painted in the new corporate blue livery but instead wasn't painted at all. The unit had its aluminium body bare of paint and just polished with red numbers and BR double arrow logos adorning the bodysides. The front was as per the 4-car units with full yellow ends complete with black surrounds to the front windows. London Underground had built later batches of their R stock units with aluminium bodies in the 1950s and a single unit was left unpainted as an experiment. It was said that by not painting the train there was not only a material cost saving but that the slightly reduced weight of not having paint would reduce running costs over the train's lifetime. The initial experiment was considered a success and from the late 1950s onward all underground trains were delivered devoid of paint with brushed aluminium bodies. BR decided to use 2001 as a test bed to see if there was merit in them following suit with their stock.

Testing of all three units continued during 1972 with the poor internal ventilation of the units being flagged up during the summer and the modification of the windows was drawn up and authorised to be completed at BREL's Eastleigh Works. The units went there in turn under their own power to have the modified windows fitted. 4001 was there during the latter half of August into September, 4002 visited during October and 2001 was the last to be modified, visiting Eastleigh in late November and emerging during the second week of December. This rolling programme ensured there remained two units back at Wimbledon for the other testing and evaluation work as the plan was to introduce them into passenger service in 1973. The units had been gauge checked to operate a limited selection of suburban lines out of Waterloo and also some routes on the Central Division out of London Bridge, but it was the former that was selected as the area that would play host to the first passenger operations of the PEP stock. The three routes from Waterloo, via Wimbledon to Chessington South, Hampton Court and Shepperton were cleared for PEP passenger operations. The latter was no surprise as it brought the unit close to its second home of Strawberry Hill EMU depot. The units had long been cleared to run in non-passenger service on other lines but it was considered prudent to limit the fare paying passenger trials to just a few routes for ease of both diagramming and the need to arrange for the rescue of the train if it got into technical trouble. The only thing capable of rescuing a PEP was another PEP, although in extreme circumstances a loco could be dispatched with the coupling match wagons that were used to haul the sets off region; there is no evidence that this ever happened.

Monday, 4 June 1973 was the date of the first passenger carrying run. Unit 4001 did the honours on its own with a trip on the Hampton Court to Waterloo line; this was only after the unit had spent the morning running empty test trips. The following day the unit worked both the down trip from Waterloo and the return from Hampton Court as a stopping passenger service; the future had arrived for British commuters. Extra trips were added over the next two weeks and then it was the turn of 4002 to make its passenger debut on June 18.

By the start of July, the test engineers and traffic management were sufficiently happy with the train's performance and reliability to diagram a full day's passenger work for a PEP train. Starting with a trip to Chessington South at 07:06 and then multiple trips to Hampton Court and Shepperton, the stock remained in service on these routes until past 23:00. Formations were mainly single 4-car at the start but 2001 made its debut in a 6-car formation and this became a regular sight over the next few weeks, there were even 8-car formations run in passenger service on several occasions. The formation varied upon the availability of units as they were sometimes required to be under maintenance or needed for other test work as well as the occasional visit to Eastleigh Works for modifications and rectification.

In a move that would never have been considered by British Railways of old, the train crew and test engineers were not the only people on the passenger runs in an official capacity; BR had engaged the services of a market research firm to get feedback from customers riding the new trains about their experience and that was compiled and sent back to both the British Rail Board and the development team to make sense of with a view to how the production trains that would be based upon these prototype units would look.

The PEP units broke new ground when they were temporarily transferred to the South Eastern Division of the Southern Region in mid-August 1973. It is believed the reason for this was to see how the trains coped with some of the busiest commuter traffic in the region, and for this they would be able to run all three units together in a 10-car formation, something that could not be done on the South Western or Central divisions where metro platforms had not been extended beyond eight carriage lengths; the South Eastern had extended to 10-car platforms during the 1950s due to their very high rush hour numbers. The routes out of Charing Cross and Cannon Street to Sevenoaks, Bromley North and Dartford (via Sidcup and Bexleyheath) were the routes cleared for this month of testing with the units being temporarily based at Slade Green depot in South East London. Again a bespoke diagram was produced for the test train and after a week of limited operation on the Sidcup and Dartford line along with crew training; the full diagram was run from 20 August with the unit leaving Slade Green Depot at just after 06:00 in the morning and returning there at half past midnight. The diagram only ran from Monday to Friday as the units were being evaluated on depot at the weekends. The trials ended on Friday, 15 September with the units back at Wimbledon on Monday 17th. The trials were not without incident and the train had brake problems on the morning of 23 August with its first service to London from Dartford which caused knock-on delays to the service throughout the rest of the morning.

During September 1973 the 4-car unit, 4002, received the B car from the 2-car unit. The reason for this swap was not apparent but it created the odd sight of two units running around with a mix and match of liveries. The coaches were swapped back again in April of 1974 but normality didn't last for long as it was then the turn of 4001 to play host to the B Car of 2001 and swap car number 64301 into unit 2001. This change became more permanent as the reformed 2-car set had a higher calling and was taken out of Southern Region traffic in August 1974 and sent back to its birthplace of York Works. The new look 4001 retained the odd silver driving car for the remainder of its passenger carrying life. Along

4002 with 4001 behind it form an eight car PEP working at Charing Cross in August 1973 during the one month trial of these units on the South Eastern division of the Southern Region. David Flett

with 4002, both units continued to provide passenger service on the same three routes as they had since June 1973. This was interspersed with occasional visits to Eastleigh Works. Significant examples of such visits occurred in February to July 1974 when bogie rectification work was carried out and again the following year when it was decided to fit two coaches of unit 4002 with experimental high backed seats. This was the last real phase of the prototype evaluation period as the first units to be constructed from the lessons learned from the PEPs were already at the design stage.

And so the test programme wound down. Both 4001 and 4002 remained in traffic until June 1976 when they were briefly towed back to Derby. After a few weeks there the decision was taken to put them both into store back at Wimbledon where they would be technically available for traffic but it is not known if they ever worked in service again after their return. By May 1977 both units were shown as no longer stored but withdrawn from traffic.

That wasn't quite the end for the pair of 4-car units as they were transferred into departmental stock, which meant they remained on the books but not in the role of revenue earning stock and could be used for other test or research purposes. Departmental units have a different numbering system to the revenue units and 4001 became unit 056 whilst 4002 became 057. In the case of the latter, the unit number on the front ends was never changed and it kept 4002 unit its last days. The silver car that was formed in unit 4001 was swapped for a blue coach from 4002 but other than that 4001 did not see much, if any, use during its departmental career. Due to the need for frequent transfers of the units between the Southern Region and Derby, the opportunity was taken to create new match wagons as the originals were in poor condition. The method of forming the train was changed, the cab ends of the unit were coupled together as these were the only Sharfenberg Schaku couplings available, the new match wagons were old four wheeled 'conflat' wagons and had the intermediate bar coupling at one end and the conventional draw gear at the other. The unit was split and re-marshalled with the cabs in middle and the match wagons coupled to the now exposed intermediate ends.

4001 was transferred from Wimbledon to Derby Railway Technical Centre where it remained until late spring of 1986 when it was sold for scrap and sent to Bird's of Long Marston where it was broken up. 4002 fared slightly better, seeing active use on two bogie test programmes. It was transferred to Derby Railway Technical Centre in August 1978 and the whole unit was painted in a new livery of grey, brown, red and blue with the last three colours ending in an up sweep before the cab ends. The livery was very similar to that applied to the prototype Advanced Passenger Trains that were on test at that time.

Car 64305 from unit 4002 after it was re liveried at the Railway Technical Centre and seen on the transverser. Colin Marsden

33 009 tows 4002 out of Clapham Yard on its way to Derby. The frequent need to transfer this unit off region lead to the creation of new translator wagons, converted from Conflats.
Colin Marsden

Close up of the conflat wagon conversion which had the buffers removed and the bar coupling added at one end to couple to the non-driving ends of the PEP stock.
Colin Marsden

With the translators coupled to the non-driving ends the cab ends were coupled together in the centre of the formation. Colin Marsden

4002 pictured on the down slow line at Wimbledon. The unit was allocated to departmental traffic by this time and although still carrying the number 4002 was on the rolling stock library as unit 057. Colin Marsden

4002 passes through Wimbledon Park District Line station bound for Wimbledon whilst on bogie test runs.
Colin Marsden

Returning to the Southern Region, still carrying unit number 4002, in the autumn of 1979, it was then operating on the Shepperton line out of Strawberry Hill depot and also on the main line between Wimbledon Park and Basingstoke to evaluate the ride and performance of a new set of bogies that were being developed by the Railway Technical Centre. It returned to Derby during June 1980, where a second set of bogies was fitted for trials which ran from September 1980 until March 1981 after which the unit was stored at Wimbledon Park Depot for nearly two years until the need for space meant it was taken to an un-electrified siding in Clapham Yard and stored there until 1990. It was clearly visible from the station and footbridge and whilst many of the thousands of commuters who used the station paid it no attention, it was something of a landmark to the many enthusiasts who knew what it was and the story it told. Then one day in June 1990 it was just towed away after sitting idle for over seven years and sent for scrapping. That was the end of the PEP story but we need to rewind and revisit the 2-car set, 2001, which was sent to York in August 1974.

Plans for the production build of units to be derived from the PEPs were in hand and the prototypes had proved the design could work on the third rail, but the new standard for main line electrification was overhead wires energised at a pressure of 25000V AC. To enable a train to work from this supply it needs to have the means to both collect the current and transform it to a lower working voltage and then rectify it to direct current. In addition, the mid-1970s were an age when British Rail's research department were embracing the concept of electronics for the new projects, which comprised not just the PEPs but the prototype of the High Speed Train and the Advanced Passenger Train. Unit 2001 had been selected as the test bed for the AC supplied version of the PEP and this involved York constructing a new intermediate car to be inserted into the unit between the driving coaches to make a 3-car set. The resultant unit was not intended to be run in passenger traffic as that part of the programme had been completed already. This new set was to develop an AC supplied unit with a new motor control system that did away with the camshaft control of the previous sets and used thyristors to regulate the flow of current to the motors. A thyristor is basically an advancement on a transistor which is a solid-state semiconductor which can allow current to pass through it to a certain level and then hold that level of flow when commanded and either increase or decrease the flow as required by the operator. Thyristors did away with the need for camshafts and being solid state had no moving parts so were considered far more reliable. They were especially suited to higher voltage applications.

The two motor coaches that now formed 2001, one blue and one silver, were fitted with new traction equipment. This came from two different manufacturers to allow

Another view of 4002 on the District Line section just beyond Wimbledon Park where the line passes the EMU depot. note the 4-SUB stabled there. The section from East Putney to Wimbledon is run by the District Line and equipped with fourth rail but wired in such a way as BR third rail trains could use it, which still happens to this day. Colin Marsden

Between test runs, 057, or 4002 as it was presenting itself, is berthed at Wimbledon Park depot. Colin Marsden

4002 and AC test unit 920 001 both pictured at the Railway Technical Centre at Derby. Colin Marsden

for a direct evaluation; one car had GEC and the other had Brush designed motors and control gear. They were fully compatible. The centre car that York built differed from the previous cars in that it only had two pairs of air operated doors per side, as opposed to three. It also had no seating inside as it was not required to carry passengers but there was provision for test engineers to use the interior of this coach and a static generator was fitted so they could power their test apparatus when the unit was not connected to a traction supply. The vehicle also had no motors, being an unpowered trailer car, but had a pantograph mounted on the roof to collect power from the AC overhead wires and a transformer under the floor to reduce the AC voltage to a lower pressure and rectify it to DC so it could power the train's traction equipment. The third rail shoegear was removed but the compressor and motor alternator were retained to provide air for the brakes and suspension and the DC and AC voltages for lighting and control circuits. The new car was painted all over blue which meant the unit still ran with one silver car as that was not repainted to match the other two. The unit was renumbered as 920 001.

What followed next for this 3-car set was an intensive programme of testing under the wires, but not until it made one final visit to the Southern Region in April 1975 when released from York, presumably as the PEP test team were based there at this time. The unit returned to Derby and from there went to its new base at Ilford in East London in July 1975. Test running took place between Colchester and Clacton with the unit returning to Ilford depot when not running. It also spent some time on the Tilbury and Southend Line before heading north to Glasgow and working on test out of Hyndland EMU Depot between March and August 1976. Over the following twelve months the unit was tested further in both Eastern and Scottish regions before ending up back at York Works in May 1978

Now applied with a black surround to the headcode display and fitted with opening top-light windows to improve ventilation, set No. 4001 awaits departure from Waterloo on 10 June 1972 with the 14.26 to Hampton Court.
Colin Marsden

and from there going into store at the Railway Technical Centre in Derby where it remained for the next nine years. In 1987, a year after 4001 was sent for scrap, the same fate befell the three coaches of 920 001 as the Railway Technical Centre sought to clear out vehicles that had no further use and were just cluttering up their yard.

With the scrapping of the last PEP vehicle in 1990, the opportunity was lost to save a vehicle for posterity, something many regret with hindsight. The PEP test programme had paved the way for what would become one of the most successful EMU families in the history of Britain's railways, but more than that they represented a coming of age for the network in how it embraced research and development which went far beyond the engineers and technicians but came to embrace the opinions of those that would be the users of the train, the customers themselves. The change to modern electronics was especially pertinent when one considers that 920 001 was put into test just under seven years after British Railways ran its last timetabled steam trains. These really were the trains of the future and could not have been any further separated from the ghosts of the past.

Following the testing and evaluation of the PEP units, the construction and delivery began for the production types based upon the experimental design. Using the lessons learned from trial running along with passenger feedback, a new standard design of suburban EMU would emerge, five classes in total. They looked pretty much alike but there were many differences in their supply, traction and control equipment that were based upon the individual demands for the routes each class were required to work. The following chapters will look at each class in the order they were constructed.

Unit 4001 leads a ten car PEP formation through Eltham Well Hall station on the line to Dartford via Bexley heath. The unpainted two car unit is in the centre of the formation with 4002 on the rear. The date of this picture is 20 August 1973 making this an early test or training run before the units started to carry passengers on this line.
David Flett

Car S64305 from unit 4002 at the Railway Technical Centre, Derby Research on Saturday 21 July 1979 with an APT behind it. Colin Whitbread

***Below left*: A close** up view of the revised livery applied to 4002. Colin Whitbread

***Below right*: The unpainted** car 64300 that was originally in the 2-car unit 2001 but by the time this photo was taken on 21 July 1979 it had been a part of three car AC test unit 920 001 for a few years. Pictured inside the shed at the RTC, the unit had been out of use for a few years. Colin Whitbread

In the period leading up to the launch of Network SouthEast, one of the PEP driving cars from set 920001, which was stored at the RTC Derby, was used for a paint style demonstration vehicle, enabling senior NSE management to decide on the final colour style. The vehicle is seen painted in an early version of NSE red, white, grey and blue, with the branding 'Operation Pride', in the EDU yard in March 1986. Operation Pride was launched by Chris Green in February 1986 in the run up to the launch of Network SouthEast. Car 64300 has clearly had all the underfloor traction equipment removed. Colin Marsden

***Below left*: 4002 spent** several years at Clapham Yard in storage following the end of its period of test use. This view was taken in 1986 and it would be there another four years before finally going away for scrap. Author

***Below right*: The interior** of 4002 in 1986. The unit had been in store for a few years and many of the cushions were removed and stacked inside. The plastic seat units and orange Formica was holding up well but this unit would never turn a wheel under its own power again. Author

Chapter 4

THE CLASS 313

The Class 313 was the first production design to follow on from the PEP. A total of sixty-four 3-car units were built with the intention of using them to equip the newly electrified suburban lines out of King's Cross to Welwyn Garden City and Hertford North which was the southern section of the Great Northern Electrification project that had been authorised by government in August 1971. Electrification out of King's Cross had been an aspiration of the 1955 Modernisation Plan but the budget wouldn't run to it, so it had gone on the wish list. The proposals went further than the lines envisaged for the 313s and included a northern phase II from Hertford North and Welwyn Garden City to Royston. It also had a Southern branch from Finsbury Park over a line currently operated by London Underground which ran in wide diameter tube tunnels from Moorgate to Drayton Park, opened as the Great Northern & City Railway. The plan allowed for the construction of a link from Drayton Park to the main line at Finsbury Park station. The lines out of King's Cross were operated by a mix of 1950s diesel multiple units and loco hauled passenger trains comprised of suburban Mark I compartment stock hauled by class 31 locomotives and they already ran to Moorgate but via a tunnel on the eastern side of King's Cross station which the new proposals would render redundant. The hope was to have the Moorgate section and the Hertford and Welwyn lines ready by late 1975 with the electrification of Finsbury Park to King's Cross ready by early 1977, the Royston section, for which a fleet of slam door EMUs based on the Mark II carriage was being built would not open until late in 1977. The electrification on the surface lines would be by overhead wires at 25000V AC with the tunnel section from Drayton Park to Moorgate changed from the London Underground 660V DC four rail system to the BR standard 750V DC third rail. This meant that the new units would have to be able to operate from both supply systems, something that had never been done before in Britain.

The design work for the 313 began in 1972 with the order placed in 1973. Construction was to be carried out at BREL's York Works and began in 1975. The electrification work was running behind schedule so the first units did not emerge until 1976. When they did it was clear that the PEP ancestry had been followed with many features carried over. The body, which would be common to all the production classes, was again aluminium with the steel underframe mounted integral to it. The lower bulge and taper of the body profile was also present as was the flat roof. This feature would be a requirement for the stock that was to run in the restricted clearance of tunnels. The cab front was different with a flatter appearance and the middle escape door was still there but positioned between two structural uprights and thus not so recessed from the two halves of the cab front. The bodysides featured only two pairs of bi-parting air operated doors on all three coaches and internally the layout was for seating bays and not airline seats inside. The half height moulded plastic units had prevailed with the detachable back and base cushions. Fluorescent lighting, public address and pressure ventilation was also provided but all windows had a hinged hopper section on their upper quarter that could be opened back into a restricted pocket to allow for extra ventilation. A 3-car unit provided 232 seats, all second class but the provision for standing passengers was carried over from the PEPs. The lobby at each driving end was still present with a single leaf door for platform access that was for crew use only and the driving cab was in the left hand side of the lobby with a power controller along with a brake controller for the three step Westcode brakes. On the roof of the middle car was the Stone Faiveley pantograph for collecting the overhead AC voltage.

Underneath, the unit had air bags for secondary suspension but the primary suspension from the axle boxes was achieved by hard rubber bushing with vertical hydraulic dampers. The air suspension was again self levelling using the same system as fitted to the PEPs. Weight distribution along the length of the 3-car set was achieved by locating different equipments to each car. Driving motor car 'A' had the compressor mounted along with the associated main air tanks whilst driving motor car 'B' had the motor alternator set and batteries fitted to it, the motor alternator had three separate outputs; 110V DC for control, emergency lighting and battery charging, 240V AC for main lighting and 415V AC for pressure heating and ventilation. In addition, each of these coaches were fitted with four GEC traction motors on each axle, each rated at 110hp and controlled by the same camshaft and resistance system as per the PEP but with some simplification that did away with the electronic logic circuits as they showed no advantage over the electromechanical logic system employed on the camshafts of CIG and VEP stock.

There were eighteen individual steps between starting and full power when motoring. The centre car had no traction motors but it did have the transformer and rectifier set between the bogies. To collect power from the third rail, the inner bogies only of each driving car were fitted with collector shoes on each side with radial arms from the bogie centres and a wooden beam to prevent the arm riding up too high if the suspension bottomed out for any reason. There was no bus line to link the individual pairs of shoes as tunnel fire regulations on the Moorgate section prevented this. The weights of each car were: DM 'A' 35.87 tonnes; DM 'B' 37.55 tonnes; and centre trailer 31.28 tonnes. The unit was designed with a maximum operating speed of 75mph. The Westcode brake was carried over from the PEP and was again a three step version but as before rheostatic braking was employed on the motor coaches, controlled by the traction camshaft, with the friction brake blended in to match on the trailer car; at lower speeds all three vehicles were reliant on the friction brake. The redesigned front ends did away with a two digit head code, which was a Southern Region thing anyway. Above the driver's window was a single destination blind whist above the non-driving side cab window were four individual blinds that together could display the 4-character alpha/numeric train reporting number. These blinds were back lit by fluorescent tubes.

The lower front end and a marker and tail lamp each side with a high intensity headlamp mounted on the driver's side only. The idea of this was to make an approaching train more visible to staff working on the track. The Scharfenburg Schaku couplers of the PEP were gone in favour of an American product known as the tightlock coupler. This was an automatic knuckle type coupling that was a development from the buckeye whereby the jaws of the knuckle locked shut when engaged ensuring a secure coupling between vehicles. There was also a locating horn on either side, one positive, one negative to ensure the coupler was properly aligned when coupling. The release of the knuckle could be carried out by a push button in the cab operating an air piston. Below the knuckle was an electrical terminal block with the air connections and brass studs for through electrical connection between units and the cover of this automatically slid out of the way during coupling and then slid back into place when the units were uncoupled. The use of this coupler on the 313s was a first for Britain and it would go on to become the standard coupling on EMUs in the country for the next twenty years. Again there were no buffers and all buffing forces were absorbed by the drag-box of the tightlock coupler.

The passenger doors reverted to the revised type of operation fitted to the PEP with the passengers pulling the doors to get them to open or close but the guard having the master release and door close function on their control panel. The units were all turned out in the BR blue and grey livery with yellow cab fronts with black surrounds to the front windows, all the underfloor equipment was in black.

By far the biggest challenge when designing the 313 was managing the change from third rail DC to overhead wire AC power supply. The units spent most of their time operating under AC conditions with the pantograph raised and the

313 033 on display at an Open Day held at Stratford TMD on 14 July 1979. Malcolm Batten

current flowing into the transformer and rectifier on the centre trailer where it was converted to 750V DC and distributed to the motor coaches to power the motors. As mentioned, these bus lines were not allowed to be energised when on the third rail so each motor coach had to be fed and act independently when the pantograph was down and third rail was supplying the train. The changeover point from one system to the other was at Drayton Park station. When at a stand at this location a power changeover switch was operated by the driver and the pantograph lowered, or raised if changing from DC to AC. The DC shoegear was permanently down and had no facility to retract. The DC shoegear would then supply the motor coaches and their associated traction and auxiliary equipment but prior to this when running into Drayton Park an automatic power control magnet was provided which tripped a circuit breaker on the train meaning the train could only continue if switched to DC mode. In the reverse direction no such facility was possible and it was all on the driver to remember to change from DC to AC. A warning signal was provided but this was unable to fail safe in the event of any driver error.

The first 313s came south to Hornsey depot in February 1976. The new service had been delayed as it was not just about new trains and electrification but the rebuilding of stations and the huge task of remodelling the approaches to King's Cross station. but was expected to start with the summer timetable with through running to Moorgate only, twelve months later the remodelling and electrification of King's Cross was completed and in 1978 the full extent of the Great Northern Electrification scheme was completed.

313s settled into their new life with comparative ease, even allowing for the usual problems associated with the introduction of new stock but the passenger operated air doors were a cause for concern with instances of doors being forced open before the train had stopped. From March 1977 the units started to undergo modification to have this function removed and the opening and closing of all doors placed under the control of the guard with individual open and close push buttons being fitted in due course. The units had complete monopoly of the Moorgate services as the only stock fitted for third rail operation, the line from Drayton Park to Moorgate had a maximum speed of 30mph so the 313s were officially limited to this when operating under third rail conditions but were capable of higher speeds. Trains were formed of either a single 3-car unit or two units in multiple. 313s did have a few peak hour diagrams into and out of King's Cross and also did occasionally venture further north than Hertford North and Welwyn Garden City, but the outer suburban work was normally the preserve of the 312 units. This could have been the story of their life for the next few decades but the 313 was to become a very well-travelled class.

Being the first of the BREL '72 family of units to enter service, the 313s were ideal for paving the way for their cousins that would be built after them. Three units were temporarily moved to the Merseyside third rail area in the second half of 1977, working out of Hall Road depot. The units concerned were 313 003/013/063. The purpose of this visit was not to supplement the operational fleet but to carry out gauging and clearance tests ahead of the delivery of the 507 fleet and also to allow for performance tests against the existing timetable and technical testing of the shoe gear and current draw on the third rail equipment. This was only a brief visit and the units returned to Hornsey

313010 leads a 6-car service on a service for Moorgate near Potters Bar, 1977. Malcolm Batten

depot after a few weeks. A more permanent change of location was on the cards a few years later.

The London Midland Region operated third rail services out of London's Euston station toward Watford Junction, including a limited service on a branch line from Watford to Croxley Green. In addition they had responsibility for the North London Line from Richmond to Broad Street station on the east side of the City of London. These lines had been operated by class 501 slam door EMUs since the late 1950s and there was a need to replace them as they approached 30 years of service. The diagramming of the 313 fleet working out of Moorgate had created a surplus of units which would release sixteen 313s for transfer to the London Midland. They would need some modification to work the new services as the single shoe per coach with no connecting bus line would create problems on the complicated track out of Euston and Richmond where there were many gaps in the conductor rail to allow for point work. To overcome this, the selected units, 313 001-016, were put through a modification programme whereby additional collector shoes were fitted to the bogies under the cab ends and these were connected to the shoes on the rear bogie of the same coach with a bus line meaning that it only required one of the four shoes on either of the driving coaches to be in contact with the live conductor rail for that coach to be capable of traction power. In the case of the leading bogie on the driver's side, there was already a shoe beam of sorts fitted which carried the tripcock equipment needed for working in tunnels. This was an air valve that would be opened if a train passed a signal that was at danger. Adjacent to the signal was a pneumatic arm that would only lower if the associated signal was showing a proceed aspect. It was used on both the Drayton Park to Moorgate lines and the section of the Euston to Watford Junction line that was shared with London Underground Bakerloo Line trains and also the Richmond to Broad Street line which was shared at the Richmond end with the District Line. The shoes fitted to the leading bogies were the same as those on the inner ends with radial arms from the bogie centre and a height limiting bar to prevent them riding up if the suspension bottomed out.

The units first entered service from 1984 on the Euston to Watford line, their use on the Richmond to Broad Street route was limited to a few trains to Broad Street from the Watford Junction line as the bulk of the services from Richmond were provided by 2-EPB units drafted in from the Southern Region and fitted with window bars due to the tight clearances in some tunnels. A 313 did have the honour of working the last service from London Broad Street when it closed in 1986 and from that year the service was extended to North Woolwich when the line to there from Dalston was electrified with the third rail. Over time, the 2-EPBs were removed from the route and the 313s took over all services. The pool of units was increased from sixteen to twenty-three, units 313 017, 019–023 and 034 made the switch from the Eastern Region and were fitted with the extra shoegear. The modified units were unable to work Moorgate to Drayton Park so to ensure they were kept in a separate pool from those on the Eastern Region the fleet was renumbered into a 313/1 subclass with the fourth digit of the unit number changed from a zero to a one. Over the following years some sections of the North London Line were upgraded due to demand for electrified freight traffic and the third rail was replaced with 25000V AC catenary. This presented no problem for the 313/1s as they retained their dual voltage capability. The units were also employed from time to time on the Watford Junction to St. Albans Abbey branch line which was also electrified with AC overhead wires.

One other temporary allocation of 313s occurred when four units were loaned to the Clacton area in 1987. This first happened due to a shortage of other units while bogie faults on the existing main line fleet was investigated and the four 313s provided temporary cover. Shortly after, 313 061-064 (the last four units built) were drafted back to Clacton in 1987 to work the local stopping services between Colchester and Clacton along with Walton-on-the-Naze. These units had their shoe gear removed for the period of their stay, including the trip cocks and beams on the leading bogies as they were only required to work on AC power. After less than a year they were returned to their regular duties and the shoegear was refitted.

Until 2010 the extent of regular 313 operations had settled down to the original lines out of Moorgate and King's Cross along with the former London Midland routes from Euston to Watford and Richmond to Stratford, as the section from

313 009 at Stonebridge Park with Watford Junction-Euston train. 30 September 1985. Malcolm Batten

313 015 in original blue and grey livery, the additional shoe gear that was needed for these units to work the Euston to Watford line is visible on the bogie nearest the cab. Peter Hoskins

there to North Woolwich had been closed to make way for an extension of the Docklands Light Railway. The routes had been supplemented by the addition of a Clapham Junction to Willesden Junction service which had been introduced to replace the former peak hours only shuttles between Clapham Junction and Kensington Olympia. The new service ran all day and again the 313s were able to use their dual voltage capability as a short section from North Pole Junction to Willesden Junction had been equipped with AC overhead wires; the rest of the line was DC third rail.

The 313s were now over 30 years old and thoughts were turning to their replacement. Since the privatisation of British Rail in the 1990s, the 313s had been owned by Eversholt Leasing who leased them to whoever operated the franchises responsible for the services they worked. The former London Midland lines had fallen under the control of Transport for London (TfL) from 2007 and they were committed to replacing the 313 units but before they did they made changes to the interior by removing some seats. This was effected by changing many of the three a side seating bays to two a side and the effect was to create even more standing room. In preparation for taking over the routes, TfL had placed an order for twenty-four 3-car class 378 'Capitalstar' units from Bombardier at Derby. The delivery of these was scheduled to start in 2008 and a target of 2010 was set for the total replacement of the 313 fleet. Deliveries of 378 units continued at a steady pace and they were commissioned and the requisite crew training carried out at such a pace that the 313s could be steadily withdrawn during late 2009 with the last booked diagrams being on 19 February 2010. After that date a handful of units were on standby use but they were stood down by the end of September that year and that was end of 313 operations on the former London Midland lines, but not the end of all the 313s that comprised their fleet. In a move that took everyone by surprise, nineteen of the 313/1s were sold by Eversholt to a new rolling stock leasing company known as Beacon Rail, formed in 2009, and had identified a further use for the 313 fleet. A twentieth unit, 313 121, was also sold to Beacon Rail but would see further use in a different role that will be covered later. The units 313 101–117 & 119–120 were refurbished in a joint exercise between Wabtec at Doncaster, Wolverton works and final modifications being made by Southern, the train operating company that ran the South Central franchise, at the Stewarts Lane depot in Battersea. What resulted from this was a new subclass of 313/2 with the units again being renumbered, this time by having the fourth digit changed from a one to a two. The units were to run on the third rail only and so their pantographs were removed, the transformers were retained as they were part of the centre cars and to shed that much weight would have meant the vehicle would have become unstable. The units also had 750v DC bus lines fitted along their entire length along with sockets so they could work from the overhead DC trolley wire systems in Selhurst and Brighton maintenance depots. The interior got a full refit, with the original half back seating removed and replaced with high back seats in 2 + 2 configuration and mainly bays of four. The seats were of the same style as fitted to Southern's class 377 'Electrostar' fleet with the exception of the seats on the bulkheads of the rear of each end that had to be an adapted low backed version due to the need to keep access to the equipment cupboards that contained circuit breakers and relays for the train's operation.

A new public address system was fitted with automated announcements and dot matrix displays, new carpets were fitted to the interior which was a first for a 313 unit, as was the provision of cab cooling and traction sand equipment. The units were painted in Southern's green and white livery with full yellow ends and were dispatched to Brighton for crew training. The first units entered service on the Brighton to Sleaford line in May 2010 and units were brought into traffic on Coastway services between Brighton, Hove, Littlehampton, Bognor Regis and Worthing during the Summer 2010 timetable, when the full fleet of nineteen 313/2 units diagrams were produced that took them as far afield as Portsmouth Harbour on stopping services to and from Brighton. Their introduction was not well received by local rail user groups who saw a train that was over 30 years old, had no on-board toilet, no air conditioning and had replaced newer stock as poor service to the customer. Many enthusiasts were taken aback at the idea of a train produced for the London commuter services now working by the coast.

With the introduction of 313s to Southern Coastway services, the fleet size remained at the original number, three of the units previously operated by TfL were transferred to join the forty one units that remained in use on their original routes on what was now classed as part of the Thameslink Great Northern Franchise. The units had to have the extra shoes removed to comply with the tunnel working requirements of the Drayton Park to Moorgate section but they were not renumbered back from their 313/1 subclass.

In 2014 the Thameslink & Great Northern Franchise was again re-let, this time as a management contract to provide the passenger service. It was awarded to Govia Thameslink Railway and included the Thameslink, Southern and Great Northern routes to make one of the largest intensive operating areas of any rail franchise. One of the terms of the new contract was that the incoming operator would replace the 313 units on the former Great Northern service, but not the coastway routes which they also operated. By this time, the 313s were 40 years old. Siemens were the preferred bidder for the new units which were classified as class 717 and comprised of twenty-five 6-car sets, constructed in Germany. Deliveries of the new stock started in the summer of 2018 and by the spring of 2019 the first units were ready to enter service. The programme to replace the 313s went relatively quickly with the first unit withdrawn in February 2019 and the last timetabled passenger run for the class being on 30 September with the 23:33 Hertford North to Moorgate service, with the stock running empty back to Hornsey depot from Moorgate, thus bringing an end to the forty-three year story of the class on the Great Northern Electrics. A week prior to the end, a railtour had been run over the routes using 313 134 (ex London Midland) and 313 064 (the last unit built). For the tour, one coach

313008 at Dalston Junction with a morning train from Broad Street to Watford Junction, 13 June 1986.
Malcolm Batten

of 313 064 was wrapped in vinyl depicting the Network SouthEast livery the units ran in during the 1980s and '90s. There was to be no reprieve for the units and one by one all were towed away to scrap yards and broken up.

This left the Coastway 313s as the last passenger outpost for the class. They were not popular for the reasons already given but they went through a C6 overhaul during 2017/8 which saw new LED lighting fitted as well as a refresh of the interior and repairs to the air system. During this programme the original 313 unit, by now numbered 313 201 was repainted into a version of the original British Rail blue and grey livery with the concession to modern accessibility regulations that required the passenger doors contrast to the rest of the body the doors were painted grey for their full height. The unit became something of a local celebrity and even had its own Facebook fan group. The 313s continued operating into the 2020s, by now the oldest mainline stock on the national network. Once the network had settled down after the Covid pandemic of 2020/21, Southern re-evaluated its rolling stock requirements and how to get best use out of its fleets. It decided to part with the older classes of 455 and 313 and concentrate on its 377 Electrostar units. After the 455 fleet was withdrawn from service in 2022, it was only a matter of time before the end came for the 313s. A charity railtour using celebrity 313 201 and 213 ran on 29 April 2023 covering all of the routes around Brighton and the south coast. The final timetabled 313 passenger run was the final Sleaford to Brighton service on the evening of Friday 19 May 2023. Over the next month, all nineteen units made the journey from Brighton and Hove to Eastleigh Works where they were all scrapped on site, with the exception of 313 201 which found salvation in preservation, that will be covered in a later chapter.

313002 at Broad Street towards the end of the station's existence. Only a basic platform was in use here for passengers to disembark on arrival from Watford. 24 October 1985.
Malcolm Batten

As part of the deal which allowed the closure of Broad Street station and the site's redevelopment, a spur was installed at Graham Road, Hackney that enabled trains from the North London line to run into Liverpool Street. A few peak hour trains ran from Watford Junction to Liverpool Street via this routing which opened on 30 June 1986. On 9 October 1987, because of engineering work, these trains were diverted to Stratford instead. 313016 waits for departure from Stratford low level with the blinds correctly set for the return journey. Liverpool Street–Watford Junction services were withdrawn on 28 September 1992.
Malcolm Batten

313063 at Colchester St. Botolphs (later Colchester Town) with a stopping service to Clacton, 18 April 1987. The unit was on loan to the Great Eastern lines and the shoe gear has been removed. This unit had an unfortunate accident at Walton-on-the-Naze on 12 August 1987 when it crashed through the stop blocks and demolished the gents' toilets, it was eventually repaired.
Malcolm Batten

313 003 was the first of the class painted in Network SouthEast livery. The original version had no black window surrounds but the central escape door was black. Pictured here at Watford Junction. Peter Hoskins

313 003 did get a later application of NSE livery with the black window surrounds but this version of the livery still has the angled up sweeps at the cab ends. Watford Junction 19 September 1989. Malcolm Batten

313 001 works the penultimate service out of Broad Street station on 27 June 1986, the 18:19 to Watford Junction. Peter Lindop

313 050 approaches Enfield Chase with train for King's Cross 9 April 1994. Malcolm Batten

313 005 passes the now demolished signal box at Camden Road 16 August 1990. Malcolm Batten

313 001 approaches Homerton on 27 February 1990. Running on third rail but with 25kv overhead wires now also installed for electric freight trains, in due course the third rail equipment would be removed. Malcolm Batten

313 011 arrives at Euston with a service from Watford Junction. There were a few DC only platforms reserved for these services amongst the masses of AC overhead wires. Author

313 021 at Brondesbury Park with a North London Line service 23 June 1994. Malcolm Batten

313 019 approaching North Woolwich, despite the headcode blind saying Stratford. The section between North Woolwich and Silvertown had been singled in later years 7 November 1999. Malcolm Batten

Pictured arriving at the rebuilt Clapham Junction bound platform at Kensington Olympia 313 009 slows for the station stop with a service from Willesden junction. Author

The transition between DMU and EMU working on the Clapham Junction to Willesden service. 313 016 departs Kensington Olympia bound for Clapham Junction passing DMU 117 704 which is on a service from Clapham Junction. 24 September1996.
Malcolm Batten

313 011 at platform 2, Clapham Junction with train for Willesden Junction 4 October1996.
Malcolm Batten

In 1989 the dual-voltage class 313s replaced the 2-EPB units on the North Woolwich-Richmond service. 313 015 enters Highbury & Islington station on the DC lines. Note the single line to the right, with overhead wiring, used by freight trains between Stratford and Willesden. 16 August 1990. Malcolm Batten

The Silverlink franchise took over the suburban services out of Euston on 7 February 1997. The company was owned by National Express and used this distinctive purple, green and white livery on all of its units. 313 022 at West Brompton 8 June1999. Malcolm Batten

A view of 313 022 this time departing West Brompton. Silverlink had not only the main lines but also all of the North London Line and this, the West London Line as part of its empire. Malcolm Batten

313 117 recently renumbered to differentiate it from the 313s working on the Great Northern. Pictured here at Richmond with a service bound for North Woolwich. Author

The very last passenger train on the North Woolwich line. A special ran after the closure of normal passenger services and was worked by unit 313101. 10 December 2006. Malcolm Batten

313 108 stands at Custom House. Interchange is available with the Docklands Light Railway, which runs alongside the line. Access is via the new footbridge which also gives access to the Excel exhibition centre which is alongside the station. 6 March 2006. Malcolm Batten

313 110 at the rebuilt Stratford station with a train from North Woolwich to Richmond 11 June 2002.
Malcolm Batten

313 104 at North Woolwich. The new station building which opened in 1979 is out of sight to the right of the old station. The building and the track to the left of the fence is the North Woolwich Old Station Museum. This opened in 1984 and was closed in 2008 1 May 2006.
Malcolm Batten

A number of units, both diesel and electric, were painted in liveries promoting the bid by London to host the 2012 Olympics. 313 120 was one such and is seen in 'Back the Bid' livery at Clapham Junction on 31 May 2005.
Malcolm Batten

First Capital Connect took over the running of the Thameslink and Great Northern services on 1 April 2006. They applied a simple blue livery to their fleet at first as worn by 313 061 at New Southgate 18 November 2006.
Malcolm Batten

The later FCC Great Northern livery was more colourful with vinyl graphics on the lower bodyside. 313 050 is seen here wearing that colour scheme at Alexandra Palace, but after the franchise ended. 1 April 2019.
Malcolm Batten

The new franchise operators made no attempt to re-livery the 313 fleet as they were committed to getting rid of them. 313 040 has a graphic to signify the new franchise but is still in FCC 'Dynamic Lines' colours here at Grange Hill 24 March 2019.
James Pickering

313 018 remained the lowest numbered unit to remain on the Great Northern lines and is seen here at Grange Hill on 24 March 2019.
James Pickering

313 029 calls at Grange Hill with a Moorgate bound service on 24 March 2019.
James Pickering

***Above left*: On 23 September** 2019 the Great Northern 313 farewell railtour ran and one vehicle of 313 064 was wrapped in a vinyl recreation of the Network Southeast livery. Pictured here at Hertford North sidings. James Pickering

***Above right*: The 313** farewell tour at King's Cross suburban platforms. James Pickering

***Right*: A close** up of the re-liveried car of 313 064 at King's Cross. James Pickering

313 217 wearing Southern livery at Newhaven Harbour on 3 June 2021. Author

Under stormy skies, 313 219 enters Ford with a service from Littlehampton to Bognor Regis with only days left in service. 10 May 2023 Author

***Above left*: 313 220** calls at Worthing with a Brighton bound service on 2 December 2021. Author

***Above right*: The refurbished** interior of a Southern 313 unit. Author

***Right*: With not** long left in service, 313 206 was still working hard, pictured here at Lewes with a Brighton to Sleaford service. 10 May 2023. Author

313 204 pictured at Bognor Regis about to work back with the 15:05 service to Littlehampton 3 June 2021. Author

On 29 April 2023 a farewell railtour for the Southern 313s was run, celebrity repainted unit 313 201 was one half of it and seen here at Littlehampton whilst the itinerary took a break for lunch. Author

The other unit used on the farewell tour was 313 213 which lead out of Littlehampton after the lunch break. Author

The furthest west the 313s ever got was Portsmouth Harbour so it was fitting that the farewell tour visited this station. James Pickering

Before leaving the story of the 313s, mention needs to be made of the twentieth unit sold by Eversholt to Beacon Rail; 313 121. This unit was not included in the Southern passenger fleet but instead made its way into the services of Network Rail as they needed a unit that could be a test bed for the European Rail Train Control System (ETCS), a form of in cab signalling that was being rolled out on Thameslink core route and also the lines out of King's Cross toward Peterborough. The 313 was to be fitted with all the in cab interfaces, which meant a new driver's instrument console was fitted. Some of the original low back seating was removed to make way for engineer's test equipment and a kitchen and toilet for when the unit ran long periods overnight between the passenger service. The original traction equipment from its Watford line days was not altered so it retained both DC and AC capability. The conversion work was carried out at Wembley Depot by Alstom and it was repainted into an all-over yellow livery with Network Rail branding. The unit spent nearly five years on the ETCS test programme from July 2013 until May 2018 when it was stored at Eastleigh works. It was eventually moved into store on the former Railway Technical Centre test track at Old Dalby where it was put up for sale. The unit received the designation of the Railway Heritage Designation & Advisory Board (RHDAB) in 2023 and was thus required to be offered for preservation. This happened for 313 121 and that story will be covered in a later chapter.

The farewell tour upon arrival back at Brighton where the day ended with 313 201 leading the final leg. The units would have a few more weeks of regular service left after this date. Author

313 121 in its Network Rail yellow livery pictured at Selhurst depot. It visited this location from time to time to use the wheel lathe. Chris Thorn

The redesigned driver's desk on 313 121 with the ETCS interface in the centre. Chris Thorn

***Below left*: The interior** of 313 121 showing where some seating had been removed and test equipment installed in its place. The seating that remained was the original plastic half back seats from the units' construction. Chris Thorn

***Below right*: This was** the rear of the interior of one of the driving cars of 313 121 with most of the seating removed for large units part of the ETCS programme. Chris Thorn

The exterior of 313 121 was largely unmolested, unlike large areas of the interior. David Silman

Chapter 5

THE CLASS 507

The second fleet to emerge in the BREL '72 family were the class 507s. Unlike the 313s the story of these is much simpler as they never left the network they were built for. The 507s were delivered to work the 'Link Line' or 'Northern Line' on Merseyside. This was created as a redevelopment of the line that ran from Liverpool Exchange to Southport and had been electrified by the Lancashire and Yorkshire Railway in 1904. Ironically it had been recommended for closure in the Beeching report with the expectation that local buses could take up the traffic, that suggestion just sounds ridiculous with the benefit of hindsight. It was also another suggestion of the report that 'it may well be up to the municipal authorities to work with both the rail and bus industries to produce a 'co-ordinated system of services' and on Merseyside this had come to fruition with the creation of the Merseyside Passenger Transport Authority which gained power from the 1968 Transport Act. The Local Government Act of 1972 had created, amongst other things, the Merseyside County Council, a new metropolitan county. This injection of local governance over local transport and the power to make change happen had seen a scheme put in place to rebuild the commuter railways in the city centre. In the case of the Southport line this meant the closure of the grand old Liverpool Exchange station and the continuation of the line in a mix of new and re-purposed tunnels which emerged south of the city centre and connected to the line which ran to Hunt's Cross. All of this was electrified to the same standard as the existing Southport line and used the BR standard of 750V DC third rail. The stock working the line was of pre-war vintage, built by the London Midland and Scottish Railway (LMS) and whilst the 502 units, as they were by then known, had been a futuristic design in the 1940s. Now over 30 years later they were certainly due for replacement.

The initial order was for forty-seven class 507 units but this was amended several times and the final number ordered was thirty-three. As they were essentially to be DC only variants of the class 313s, this meant lead time in their construction was seriously reduced. The same BREL '72 family bodyshell and running gear as per the 313 was used with the units being built on the same assembly line at BREL's York Holgate Street works. The 3-car layout was identical to the 313s' with both driving cars motored on each axle but with no need for a pantograph or transformer/rectifier, the centre trailer car was considerably lighter than the other two, coming in at just over 25.5 tons compared to the 37 tons of the B end driving car that had the motor alternator and back up 110V batteries fitted. The other driving car was designated the A end and that had the compressor and main air tanks fitted and weighed in at just over 35.5 tons. Inside, the seating was the same half backed units as the 313, the lobby and driving cab layout was the same and the rheostatic and westcode friction brakes were exactly as per the 313. The motors were also controlled by a pneumatic camshaft. Current collection was by collector shoes mounted on the rear bogies of each driving car but a bus line connects these through the centre trailer to reduce the risk of a unit getting gapped over junctions and complex pointwork with plenty of breaks in the conductor rail. The non driving side of each leading bogie also has what appears to be a shoebeam but it is where the tripcock device is fitted as these had been in used on the Mersey electric network for a number of years and the new generation of stock was to continue with that tradition. It should be noted that it was fitted on the same side to the ones fitted to 313 units. One change to the 313 design was the absence of the passenger 'pull to open' doors. The doors on the 507s were all released by the guard at stations in unison and there were no individual door open or close buttons provided at the doors themselves.

The first unit was delivered from York to Birkenhead North depot, on the Wirral line, in September 1978. The head start of having had the 313 units on the network to do the clearance tests just under a year previously meant that the units could be put out on test almost immediately as there were no clearance issues and the first test and training runs were undertaken early in October 1978. Such was the confidence in their new units that during the afternoon of 25 October, units 507 001 and 002 were coupled together and ran a special service from Moorfields to Kirkby conveying HM The Queen (she rode in unit 001) and invited dignitaries. Her Majesty had unveiled a plaque at Moorfields prior to boarding the train to mark the completion and official opening of the Merseyrail Underground System.

On 1 November unit 507 001 worked its first passenger services on the Southport line with unit 507 002 working the same day on the Ormskirk line. The delivery, commissioning and introduction of the remaining thirty-one units was rapid and by the start of the May 1980 Summer timetable the whole fleet was in service with the last 502 units taken out of traffic the following September as 507 reliability had reached the expected levels.

The fleet was reduced to thirty-two units after a serious collision on 30 September 1991 when 502 022 was written off following a collision at Kirkdale depot. The damaged unit was towed to Llandudno Junction where it was stored in the carriage shed there. The undamaged driving car found further use, more of which later, but the remainder of the unit was eventually scrapped. The intention had been from the outset to keep the 507 units on the Northern line with the later built 508s being exclusive to the Wirral route. By 1997 and the advent of rail privatisation this policy was officially abandoned and it became more frequent to see the 507s on the Wirral and vice versa. The class was given a full refurbishment from 2002 with each unit taking a turn to visit Eastleigh Works where it was fitted with new 2+2 high back seating, CCTV and dot matrix passenger information displays. The biggest change was to the front end where the headlight/marker/tail light units which had been arranged horizontally were replaced with integral units which featured a headlight and a combined LED marker/tail light unit which were fitted in a unit that slanted towards the centre of the cab at an angle of 45 degrees and earned the nickname of cat's eyes. The refurbishment programme was completed during 2005. A second unit was written off in an accident on 13 March 2021 when 507 006 collided with the buffer stops at Kirkby station and took several weeks for the damaged car to be recovered. By this time withdrawal of the class was imminent so it was not repaired but sent for scrap.

Perhaps the most important thing to bear in mind about the 507s, much like the other classes built in this family of units, was how unremarkable they were; and that isn't said with any disrespect. The fleet literally turned up each day, put in a shift, went back to the depot and then did it all again the next day. Once their new status changed to that of everyday they became a part of the daily fabric of life for the cities they served. Their reliability was always good and as they never strayed from their native Merseyside the staff who worked on them knew them very well, perhaps even the individual foibles of each unit. But nothing lasts forever and as long ago as 2014 the Liverpool Metropolitan Region had set out a strategic transport plan that included its desire to replace both the 507 and the 508 units. In 2015 companies were invited to tender for the replacement fleet with the winning bidder being announced as Stadler Rail the following year. However, the design and construction process was not as swift as that which had seen the 507s created. It would be early 2020 when the first class 777 units were delivered from Stadler and the test programme was further delayed by the need for considerable infrastructure changes. The first passenger carrying run of a 777 took place in January 2023.

In December 2023 pioneer unit 507 001 was repainted into an approximation of its original BR blue and grey livery with the concession of all grey doors to comply with accessibility regulations. Withdrawals of 507 units gathered pace during 2024 with more 777 units becoming available for traffic. Two farewell railtours were run for the class, both by the Branch Line Society. The first was run on 15 September

2024 and called The Wirral Swansong and used 507 001 paired with 507 003. The second tour was called The Sefton Sparkler and again 507 001 was one half of the formation but this time its running mate was 507 023. Both tours were sold out as it was the end of an era for Merseyside's rail enthusiasts. The 507s were ordinary and mundane but that is what people connected with, something that was a 'theirs', a local icon of the city, and one that was now going to pass into history. 507 units continued to be available to cover for unavailable 777s for a few more weeks and the last recorded passenger working was on 28 November 2024 when 507 003 and 029 worked the 09:02 Liverpool Central to Southport; not only was it the last 507 working it was the very last passenger run of any complete unit from the BREL '72 family.

Over the next two months the units were dragged dead from Birkenhead North depot to South Wales where they were scrapped by Unimetals at their Newport facility, all except two. Two of the driving coaches from 507 028 was moved to Merseyside Fire & Rescue Service Training School, at Aintree Fire Station where they are mounted on a short stretch of track, complete with buffer stops. Prototype unit 507 001 made the trip to Newport but it had already been saved and was only making the journey so it could be collected by road transport for the next story in its life which will be covered in another chapter.

507 002 in the original BR blue and grey seen at Hunt's Cross on 21 May 1990. Malcolm Batten

A rather sorry looking 507022, in store at Llandudno Junction carriage shed. The trailer seen here, 71363, was scrapped but the driving car nearest the camera is 64426, which was converted to a class 314 and in used in Glasgow as part of set 314 203, renumbered to 64588. David McGuire

507 028 at Kirkdale depot in 1996 wearing what was the first Merseyrail livery and applied before privatisation, hence the additional Regional Railways branding. Author

507 018 on the left with 508 131 on the right at Birkenhead North in 1997, by this time any ideas of keeping the 507s and 508s on separate sides of the River Mersey had long been abandoned. Author

Pioneer class member 507 001 enters Chester with a Wirral line service in 1998. Author

507 028 between duties at Southport July 1996. Author

Showing off the yellow variant of the Good Communications livery and its revised front end with cats' eyes lighting clusters, 507 030 enters Hooton with a service bound for Liverpool. 26 October 2023. Author

The grey side of the Good Communications livery is evident on 507 018 as it stops at Liverpool Central with a service for West Kirby. 19 November 2023. Author

A daylight view of the grey side of the Good Communications livery as worn by 507 028 at Port Sunlight on 26 October 2023. Author

507 001 was repainted into this re-creation of its original BR livery but with modern concessions to accessibility rules that required all the doors to be grey. It was used regularly on timetabled services as well as the farewell tours. Seen here at Sandhills. James Pickering

507001 at Southport preparing to depart with the Sefton Sparkler railtour on 3 November 2024. The headboard on the right is the original one that it wore on 1 November 1978 for its first passenger working. Class 507 Preservation Society

Chapter 6

THE CLASS 314

The Class 314 was the smallest class of units built in the BREL '72 family of units and like the 507s they never strayed from their home turf. They were also the shortest lived of the units in the family, but that was still an impressive service life of 40 years.

The class 314s were a direct development from the class 920 unit created from the 2-car PEP prototype. In many respects the finished unit owed a lot to the work done on that set which visited Glasgow on several occasions for extended testing. There is a mistaken belief that the 920 was a development step for the 313s due to it appearing less than two years before the 313s were introduced. This is not the case as there was nothing on the 920 that influenced the 313 concept as it was a thyristor drive on a purely overhead AC supplied platform, which was the concept for both the 314s and 315s that followed them. An outline specification for both the 314 and 315 units was issued by the British Rail's CM&EE Projects department as early as March 1975. In this document were the earliest proposals for the 314s which show how far the research and development was at the time over a year before the 313s were delivered. The concept included, amongst other things, the desire to have the motor equipment fitted to one driving car which would also host both the batteries and compressor with the centre pantograph car equipped with another four motors and the transformer, rectifier, auxiliary compressor with the other driving end being just a driving trailer car. From the outset the units were going to have thyristor traction control. A few other things that hadn't yet filtered down from the PEP testing was that the idea of passenger pull to open doors was still preferred in the specification and that the 314s were not to be fitted with rheostatic braking, but rely only on Westcode electro pneumatic friction brakes. Of course in the following four years a lot changed based on experience with the 920 and the introduction of 313s and 507 units.

Built on the usual production line at BREL's York Holgate Road works the outline and interior layout was exactly as had gone before with other builds in the family, a trailer coach with driving motor coaches either side of it to make a 3-car set. The trailer car had the pantograph on the roof with the transformer rectifier slung below the chassis which was integral to the body shell. The motor coaches had each axle powered and like all units in the family these motors could be either the GEC G310AZ or the Brush TM61-53. These motors were both rated at 110hp and despite being from different manufacturers were more or less identical and either would fit into the mountings on any BREL '72 stock motor bogie; indeed I was told that it was not unknown for a unit to have any combination of either motor in any position, even one of each on the same bogie. Unlike previous units there was no A or B end driving car as both were identical and had the thyristor drive unit and the traction motors. As the 314 had no motor-alternator, instead a 110V DC feed was tapped from the bus line output of the transformer/rectifier and that fed a battery charger that kept the batteries in a state of constant charge as long as the pantograph was connected to live overhead wires, the batteries were mounted on the centre car. The driving cars weighed in at just over 34.5 tons whilst the trailer was 33 tons. A bus line ran the length of the unit so the motor coaches could be supplied with current from the transformer rectifier. The motor control was straight out of the lessons learned from the class 920 with no camshaft controlled traction resistance but thyristor control along with the compressor and associated air tanks. The motor coaches had the usual Westcode electro pneumatic friction braking capability on all three coaches but as per the original specification, no provision was made for rheostatic or dynamic brakes.

Inside the 314s there was the usual layout of low backed 3 + 2 seating with plastic moulded bases and two pairs of air operated sliding doors with standing room around the openings. The glass draft screens had steel poles for standing passengers to hold onto, fluorescent lighting with public address and pressure ventilation assisted by the opening hopper windows. The 314s had no individual passenger door open and close buttons, only the 313s ever had the prototypical pull to open doors and this system was never fitted to another unit in the family after, the 314s relied upon the guard to open and close all the doors in unison. The 3-car unit seated 212 people. As can be garnered from this description, the 314s were standard units with all the common features of the family with the significant differences being the inclusion of thyristor motor control and the absence of rheostatic brakes.

The need for the 314 units came about due to a re-opening of a line closed in 1964 as a result of the Beeching Report which ran under the centre of Glasgow. The line was originally part of the Glasgow Central Railway and included a tunnel section. The project was a joint venture between British Rail and the Strathclyde Passenger Transport Executive. The rebuilt section linked Kelvinhaugh, north of the Clyde, through the tunnel to Rutherglen, south of the river, and thus joined up sections of Glasgow's previously electrified suburban networks. It was initially marketed as the 'Trans Clyde', but also known as the Argyle Line because it ran under Argyle Street, Glasgow's main thoroughfare, where a new station was provided simply called Argyle Street. Some other previous stations on the route were re-opened, but not all. Tying in with the project was an upgrade to the city's circular underground metro which was not linked to the national network as it was electrified with conductor rails and had a narrower track gauge. The procurement of the fleet of sixteen class 314 units was necessary as the extra services created by the Argyle Line re-opening was beyond the existing fleet of ninety-one units of class 303 and 311 that had been built for the original Glasgow suburban electrification in 1960 and subsequent extension in the mid to late 1960s. In addition to the new service the units were also to be used supplementing older stock on the North Clyde route between Aidrie and Helensburgh Central. As the 314s were fitted with tightlock couplings they had no compatibility with the older units so any failure of one in service carried a risk as it could take time to arrange a rescue which would decimate the service.

The units were numbered 314 201–216 and all were painted in the standard corporate British Rail blue and grey livery but with white 'Trans Clyde' branding on the lower bodyside near each cab. Glasgow had two EMU depots, Hyndland on the north side of the city and Shields depot on the south side. The 314s were to be based at the former and the first units were delivered from York to Glasgow in July 1979. Crew training and commissioning was undertaken out of Hyndland and progressed well. On 5 August prototype unit 314 201 was taken to be displayed at Glasgow Central Station where an open day was being held to celebrate the station's centenary. Also on show was one of the brand new APT sets. The first recorded passenger working for 314 units took place on 26 October when 314 204 + 208 worked services on the North Clyde line. The Argyle Line was officially opened by the Queen, accompanied by the Duke of Edinburgh on 1 November and the royal party travelled over the new section of railway on unit 314 210. Public passenger services commenced on the Argyle line on 5 November with nearly all the 314 units in service by this date. Class 303 and 311 units supplemented the new stock to ensure a full service could be run and this became the norm with older units continuing to operate the line in addition to 314s as both fleets were to be utilised fully over a variety of routes.

The 314 fleet settled in very quickly to their duties and reliability became quite impressive after some early teething problems were ironed out. One more serious problem occurred when 314 203 collided at low speed with 314 215 on 5 June 1980 at Hyndland junction causing damage to vehicles at each end of the units. The temporary fix was to reform a hybrid unit of the undamaged cars; two vehicles from 215 and one from 203 until the other vehicles could be repaired.

The 314s became the first BREL '72 units to lose the corporate BR blue and grey livery when Strathclyde PTE started to adorn all the stock used in their area with a new livery of orange body with black around the windows, along with 'Strathclyde Transport' branding, this was not only applied to the 314s, but the 303s, 311s and diesel units working in the Glasgow area. The first 314 repainted was 216 in August 1983 with the last one, 314 213, painted a year later. Hyndland depot closed in 1987 and the fleet was re-allocated to Shields depot along with the whole Glasgow EMU fleet. Driver only operation came to Glasgow from 1990 and the 314s were converted to operate with only a single crew member, this involved the door open and close buttons being positioned on the driver's desk which were operated in conjunction with the driver observing passengers boarding and alighting in television monitors provided in banks at stopping points along the platform.

The unlucky 314 203 was again involved in a collision at Newton on 21 July 1991 whilst working a Balloch to Motherwell service. It crashed into a class 303 unit working a Newton to Glasgow Central service on a single line section at what was estimated to be a combined speed of 60mph. Both train drivers and two passengers were killed in the impact. The wreckage was recovered and a full investigation took place that concluded that the service from Newton had started against a signal being held at danger putting it into the path of the service from Balloch. The report was highly critical of the track layout at this area and from the recommendations the junction was remodelled to make it far safer. The wreckage of both trains was removed from the site. The damaged driving motor car of 314 203, 64588, the same vehicle that had been damaged in the slow speed collision just over eleven years previously, was written off but the other two cars of the unit were repairable. In order to create a replacement for the destroyed vehicle, British Rail's engineers took an approach that showed just how sensible and flexible the idea of building a standard fleet of EMUs was. A class 507, unit 507 022, had been damaged in a collision in Liverpool and two of its remaining cars were stored at Llandudno Junction. The undamaged 507 driving car, 64426, was rebuilt with its control wiring and traction equipment so it was compatible with the 314 fleet. The interior was refitted as a test bed for future 314 facelift with new lighting diffusers, curved interior draught screen, restyled litter bins, carpets and different seating, it even had mats at the doorways to remove dirt from passengers' shoes. The vehicle was released back into traffic formed in 314 203 from 16 May 1996 with the vehicle being renumbered to 64588, the number of the vehicle it replaced. The unit was also named *European Union* and was the only 314 unit to wear a name.

Whilst all of this was happening, the 314 fleet suffered further temporary casualties in December 1994. Two units were trapped on the Argyle line when the tunnels flooded due to the River Kelvin bursting its banks. Units 314 208 + 212, coupled together as a 6-car train, were trapped at Glasgow Central low level station as the water rose to well above platform level resulting in the trains and the station being evacuated. The line was closed for a lengthy period with the units abandoned until the water levels subsided. The units were eventually recovered but the water damage was considerable and it was nearly nine months before the tunnel re-opened to normal traffic. Both units were eventually repaired and returned to traffic. The floods did not just affect the railway. Glasgow as a whole was severely impacted and it has been described as the worst natural disaster to hit the city in living memory.

By 1997 the 314 fleet was back to full strength and the Glasgow suburban electric network had considerably expanded since they had been built nearly twenty years earlier. The line to Ayr and Largs was electrified in the late 1980s along with new stock arriving to work it. Strathclyde Transport was rebranded to Strathclyde Passenger Transport and the orange and black livery was slowly replaced by a carmine red and cream livery. The first 314 to be repainted was 314 215 in August 1997 but repainting of the remaining fleet was a very long drawn out process. Rail privatisation was occurring and the Scotrail franchise, of which the PTE services were a part, were now run by a firm better known in the bus world, National Express. The orange and black livery was still to be found on five of the class 314 fleet well into the early 2000s. One 314 unit repainted into a revised second version of the red and cream livery in 2004 which had the full height of the doors painted cream so they contrasted with the red body for accessibility rules. The orange livery finally disappeared in November 2006 when 314 202 was repainted into the revised red and cream livery.

Further changes to the work allocated to the 314s came in the late 1990s with them switched to run on the Cathcart Circle line out of Glasgow Central high level station. They also made occasional trips to Gourock and Wemyss Bay. The class broke further new ground in the winter of 2009/2010 when they ventured on a few occasions to both Ayr and Largs. The whole fleet was put through a refreshment programme during 2011. The rebuilt coach in 314 203 was not to be the blueprint for this, in fact it lost its carpets and revised seating and had those features reverted to near original spec but it still retained the unusual littler bins and draught screens for the rest of its existence. The remainder of the fleet got an interior repaint, new vinyl floor covering, and new seat covers. The units were also fitted with on train monitoring recorders (black boxes) which were now a required safety feature along with the train protection and warning system equipment that had been fitted a few years previously. Five units 314 203/4/8/11/12 that were still in the original red and cream livery were repainted into a new Scotrail livery of all over blue with the saltire in white at the vehicle ends, units that were in the revised red and cream were not repainted during the refresh but 209 and 214 did get the new livery in 2017. The 314s were chosen as the preferred traction for the newly electrified Paisley Canal branch when services started in December 2012; indeed this route was to become their mainstay until their retirement with occasional work on other routes.

New legislation that demanded a certain level of features provided on public transport for persons of restricted mobility, known as the PRM requirements was going to come into effect on 1 January 2020 and ahead of this Scotrail took a look at what would be needed to make the 314s compliant. The units were by then the oldest EMUs working in the country and were

314 209 arrives at Motherwell with a local service 9 April 1981.
Bruce Galloway

starting to show their age. The fleet had never been fitted with CCTV or dedicated spaces for wheelchair users and the cost of bringing them up to spec when offset against their age and expected life span meant the 314s were to be retired in favour of a fleet of new units, built by Hitachi and classified as the 385s. Withdrawal of the class commenced in the autumn of 2018 with 314 212 being the first unit taken out of traffic and quickly cannibalised for parts to keep the remainder running. A further five units were withdrawn before the end of 2018 and in January 2019 those units began to be towed away to Glasgow Works for component recovery before going for scrap in either Kingsbury or Newport. 314 204 was taken by road to Eastleigh as TfL were interested in evaluating if the class may be suitable for use on some of their services. It proved not to be and this unit was eventually scrapped at Eastleigh in July 2020. By December 2019 only five units remained in traffic and these were gone before the end of the year. The final passenger run by a 314 was 14 December when 314 216 operated the 17:35 Paisley Canal to Glasgow Central. On Wednesday, 18 December, 314 202 + 205 operated a farewell railtour out of Glasgow Central visiting Ayr, Carstairs, Cumbernauld and Helensburgh Central, before returning to their original stomping ground of Glasgow Central low level platforms, bringing to an end 40 years of 314 operations in Scotland. Over the following months the remaining units went on their final journeys to be scrapped, with the exception of 314 209 which remained at Yoker Depot until December 2020 when it was moved to Shields depot and from there by road to Bo'ness where it was to be the test bed for a new form of electric train.

This shot of 314 213 leading a 6-car rake was taken in late August 1979 at Dumbarton Central and these brand new units were likely to have been on driver training duties. Eddie Holden

314 208 at the rear of six car service arriving at Glasgow Central. Author

314 203 car 64589 written off and replaced by ex Class 507 driving car 64426, rebuilt at Glasgow Works as a vehicle interior demonstrator showing various designs. With its former 507 vehicle nearest the camera the set is seen at Milngavie on 16 May 1996 on a demonstration run. Colin Marsden

314 204 in Strathclyde orange and black livery at Helensburgh Central.
Author

314 207 at Partick with a service for Lanark, 19 May1988.
Malcolm Batten

314 216 at Whifflet 4 June 1996 with service to Coatbridge.
Colin Marsden

314 215 at Anniesland wearing the first version of the Strathclyde carmine and cream livery, 29 July 1999.
Malcolm Batten

314 207 wearing the revised carmine and cream with the all cream doors on 28 July 2015 at Glasgow Central, working 2N02 12.05 Glasgow Central to Neilston.
Colin Marsden

314 207 on 02/07/2014 stabled between duties at Glasgow Central.
Colin Marsden

Another view of 314 207 stabled at Glasgow Central showing off its Strathclyde livery.
Colin Marsden

314 202 on 28 July 2015 at Glasgow Central with the 2P02 12.20 Glasgow Central–Newton service.
Colin Marsden

02 July 2014 314 207 at Glasgow Central, 2D31 13.42 Glasgow Central to Paisley Canal with 314 208 adjacent arrived of Cathcart Circle service. Colin Marsden

314 208 at Glasgow Central on 02 July 2014 with 1G09, 13.55 Glasgow Central–Gourock. Colin Marsden

314 204 shows of the blue 'Saltire' Scotrail livery at Glasgow Central departing with a Cathcart Circle service 02 July 2014. Colin Marsden

***Below left*: On the** final day of timetabled passenger operation of the 314s, 314 216 operated between Paisley Canal and Glasgow Central, seen here at the latter. Khai Slater

***Below left*: Another view** of 314 216 on the final timetabled day of operations, seen here at Paisley Canal. Khai Slater

The push to decarbonise rail travel in the UK had gathered pace in the 2010s with electrification being the preferred option, but that comes with a hefty price tag and options for lines where electrification cannot be provided were being explored. Batteries work but come with limitations on range and the need to be close to recharging facilities. Another option that had been trialled in the auto industry was the hydrogen cell. This used a supply of hydrogen to generate electricity which feeds the batteries that supply power to the train. The benefit is that the only by-product of burning hydrogen is water vapour. The down side is that hydrogen cells take up a lot of room and need to be refilled, rather like an internal combustion engine. 314 209 was selected as the basis for a hydrogen cell trial run in a partnership between Arcola Energy and St Andrews University. The trial would be based at the Bo'ness and Kinneil Railway, the headquarters of the Scottish Railway Preservation Society whose running line would provide a stretch to trial the capabilities of the unit which would not be trialled on the main lines due to the cost and complexity of getting an operating certificate. The conversion involved removing most of the interior from one of the driving cars and the underfloor equipment from the centre trailer so the hydrogen cell and batteries could be installed. In the remaining two coaches, new style seating was installed. The original traction motors and control equipment was removed and replacement three phase AC traction motors fitted. AC motors are smaller and draw less current that DC ones so were seen as more suitable for the test train. The unit had suffered from graffiti attacks whilst in store at Yoker and the saltire livery was cleaned up and 'Scottish Hydrogen Train' vinyl branding added to it. The unit was

A night study of the hydrogen converted 614 209 at Bo'ness station. Josh Wright

614 209 shut down at Bo'ness between tests, the Saltire livery got damaged by graffiti and had to be cleaned up, the lower bodyside had bespoke graphics added to reflect the hydrogen project. Josh Wright

also renumbered to 614 209 at both ends. The COP26 climate conference was held in Scotland in November 2021 and the unit was made available for display during that time. In March 2022 the unit made its first moves around the yard at Bo'ness under its own power and made trips over the full 5-mile line the following May. Trial running continued until the summer of 2023 after which time the hydrogen equipment was decommissioned and the unit moved by road to the site of Glasgow Springburn Works in January 2025. The site is now run by Gibson Engineering and they will undertake the removal of the hydrogen pack equipment and have stated a commitment to retain 314 209 as a training tool to assist in developing their apprentices.

614 209 at Bo'ness station, wearing a replica Haymarket depot sticker on the front, a depot they were never allocated to. Josh Wright

The 614 in daylight at Bo'ness. The thyristor equipment between the bogies has been removed and replaced with hydrogen cell equipment. The unit could only carry approx 80kg of hydrogen which would not be enough to work a shift on the main line but adequate for the short distance test trips on the heritage railway. Josh Wright

Chapter 7

THE CLASS 508

Of all the classes to be built for the BREL '72 family the class 508s have enjoyed the most varied working lives by far. Built at around the same time as the 314s, these units were very different in specification to those as they were intended for Merseyside where the intention was to use them on the Wirral lines to replace the ageing LMS built class 503 units which dated from 1938. As such they were very similar to the class 507s in that they were supplied by DC third rail only. Despite British Rail being a nationalised company, it was still run as a business with various departments of that business having their own budget responsibility with those budgets set by the British Rail Board. The funding for the 508s was taken from the London Midland Region, who paid for three coach trains. The problem came when it was apparent that the region would not be in a position to accept them straight away, due in part to the need to get the 507 units bedded in and infrastructure work on the Wirral lines. The Southern Region had a need to withdraw its ageing 4-SUB units so their motors and compressors could be reclaimed for use in the next generation of suburban stock, the class 455, that was on order for the region. The solution was to divert the 508 units to the Southern Region upon delivery, who would lease them short term so they could be utilised as replacement for a large number of SUB units until the first class 455s were ready. The problem with that plan was the 508 units were only three coaches long and the Southern Region needed 4-coach units to cope with their passenger numbers. The solution was to add an extra coach to the formation, but this had to be paid for by the Southern Region from their rolling stock budget. When the 508s were to be sent onward to Merseyside the extra trailer coach would be removed and retained by the Southern Region to be inserted into the second batch of new suburban stock that was at that time being designed under the project name of class 510. The plan was agreed by all parties and construction of the extra trailers commenced at the same time as the remainder of the 508 units at York. The initial order had been for fifty-eight 508 units but that was trimmed down to forty-three due to funding constraints. Given the hindsight of 508 utilisation on Merseyside over the following decades, the original order would have been way in excess of what was actually needed, even if some of the hoped for extensions to their network had taken place.

Whilst the units followed the exact same outline as previous BREL '72 constructions there were a few differences under the floor. The driving cars were all fitted with four traction motors with camshaft control. This also controlled the rheostatic braking on those cars, with the three step Westcode being fitted on all vehicles. It blended in on the trailers at higher speeds and all vehicles were slowed to a stop on the friction brake below a certain rail speed. This was achieved with speed probes on the axles that were also linked to the wheel slide/slip protection equipment (WSP) and electronically controlled. The system had been fitted to the PEP prototypes and became a standard feature on all of the BREL '72 family, and subsequent multiple unit types. Over the course of their lives various modifications were made and upgraded systems were swapped for the original. As built, the 508s WSP equipment, the BR Mk II version, was to prove problematic from the off and in practice was subject to a lot of refinements after some serious problems occurred when the units' logic boxes thought the train was sliding and automatically released the brakes without any intervention from the train driver. The two driving cars differed further in that one end had the batteries and motor alternator and was designated motor coach B, the other end had the compressor and air tanks and was designated motor coach A. The compressor was different to that fitted to other units in the family being an old design designated Westinghouse DH25. These compressors had been in use on EMUs since the 1930s and were both reliable and easy to maintain but they were not as efficient as the newer type of compressor fitted to the class 313s and 507s so to meet the units demand for compressed air, which supplied the brakes, doors and air suspension, a second DH25 compressor was fitted to one of the trailer cars which also has the same layout of air tanks underneath and was designated trailer A. This car was coupled to motor coach A. The other trailer car was designated trailer B and was coupled directly to motor coach B. This trailer car had no extra equipment underneath and it was this car that had been funded by the Southern Region. The collector shoes were mounted either side of the leading bogies in traditional Southern Region layout, with a bus line running the length of the unit linking the two sets of shoes together so only one shoe had to be in contact with the conductor rail for the whole unit to be live. This arrangement was absolutely the norm on the Southern Region but would not be suitable when the units went to Merseyside.

Inside the units the layout was the same as previous builds but the 508s were the first units in the family to be fitted with individual passenger door open and close buttons. A panel was mounted to the right of the doors on the inside with a circular rubber open and close button one above the other; on the outside, a single rubber open button was mounted on a square plate either side of each pair of doors. This feature would be disabled after delivery to Merseyside but the plated over door buttons remained one the most obvious visual differences between a 507 and a 508 until refurbishment. Standard low back seating units were fitted in mostly 3+2 configuration which reduced to 2+2 around the door areas to increase standing room and allow for better passenger circulation during heavy loading.

Other standard BREL '72 features were the fluorescent tube lighting, public address and pressure heating and ventilation. Like other members of the family, the whole unit was gangwayed throughout with the now standard hinged plywood doors covered in Formica facing provided at the end of the coaches to allow access to the internal gangway connections; as before, the lobby and driving cab had no gangway access to units coupled in multiple with the standard evacuation only door being in the middle of the cab front. The tightlock couplers were again fitted with the air and electrical connections in a block connector below it. The use of tightlocks was a first for the Southern Region who had used buckeye couplings on all of its stock since 1951 and so set of pins and adaptors had to be carried by all units to allow a buckeye fitted unit to couple to a tightlock fitted unit in an emergency to move it clear of the running line at slow speed in the event of a failure. The units were all painted in the standard BR blue and grey livery with yellow ends offset with black surrounds to the front cab windows. The units were numbered 508 001 to 508 043.

The completed units were towed south from York to Strawberry Hill depot in South-West London where they were to be commissioned and the engineering team responsible for overseeing this were all based at the depot. These movements involved the use of converted wagons and brake vans that acted as translators for the tightlock couplings, and the trains had to run as unfitted goods trains due to the lack of compatible braking between the 508 and the locomotive. The first units arrived in August 1979 and early test runs were made between Strawberry Hill and Shepperton with higher speed testing being carried out between Wimbledon and Basingstoke. The units were initially cleared to work the same lines as the PEP prototypes had been but with the addition of the Kingston Loop line that ran from Teddington round via Twickenham and onward to Waterloo via Richmond. In due course other routes were to be added but for the initial passenger operations the units worked just between Waterloo and Shepperton with the first public runs taking place on 17 December 1979. Training of both drivers and guard on the new stock was undertaken at the Southern Region training school located at Waterloo South Sidings. The units were not popular and crews disliked the WSP equipment that they felt took too much control of the brakes away from them. One modification that had to be made to the 508s, and indeed all of the BREL '72 family involved the traction interlock. This was the circuit that was only completed when the train detected that all passenger doors were fully closed. As built, this circuit then allowed for the guard's starting bell to be sounded, doors open or not fully closed would illuminate an orange hazard light on the upper side mid-way down the bodyside and the circuit would fail to complete, meaning the guard could not give the ready to start bell signal. It had originally been felt that this feature alone would be sufficient to prevent a train being moved without the doors being properly closed but at least one incident occurred when this did happen. A full modification of the circuit was made and in addition to preventing the signal bell being sounded. It also broke the driver's traction control circuit, meaning that if an attempt was made to take power without interlock, the brakes would still release but the train wouldn't power up. Today this is industry standard and serves to illustrate how much of a transition the introduction of the BREL '72 family was from the days of slam door trains.

During the following years, nearly all of the 508 units entered passenger service. 508 002 was the last unit to be released by the commissioning team as it was used as a test bed for WSP modifications and didn't enter service until November 1982. On 21 April 1982 unit 508 031 was forming the 06:34 Waterloo to Shepperton, when approaching the terminal

508 031 on 18 August 1980 descending the Wimbledon Flyover passing Wimbledon Park (East), with an up Chessington-Waterloo service. Colin Marsden

station at the end of the run the WSP picked up the wheels were sliding and released the brakes, the brakes failed to fully re-apply on each subsequent attempt and the unit ploughed through the buffer stops and demolished the low wall behind them before coming to rest with its cab end hanging over the end of the wall into the street at Old Charlton Lane. Thankfully no one was seriously injured but an investigation revealed that a greasy mixture that had been applied to the rails the night before whilst WSP testing was being conducted had not been properly cleaned off and this was the cause of the crash. The unit was repaired a few months later. A WSP override button was eventually fitted to the driving desks that disabled the WSP equipment if pressed and kept the brakes applied, this would be rolled out on all fleets of Westcode fitted EMUs in due course.

The first two units to be sent from the Southern Region to Merseyside were 508 042 and 043. This happened in November 1981 and the process was one that would be replicated several times over. The units had their B trailer car removed, which was put into store, and the formation was recoupled as a 3-car set. It was then held pending locomotive haulage, with the shoe gear removed. The units were towed to Birkenhead North depot where they underwent the necessary modifications to enable them to work on the tunnel network of the Liverpool Loop line. This involved fitting the shoe gear to the rear bogies of the driving cars and removing the train bus line forward of that. This kept the length of the live connection between the shoes to a minimum of just over one coach length. On the non-driving side of the leading bogie, a new beam was fitted that held the trip cock equipment, the same as fitted to the 507s. The units had their Southern Region destination blinds, which were above each cab front windows, replaced with a single destination blind above the driver's window. The one above the non driving

508 038 at Clapham Junction with a train from Shepperton for Waterloo, 5 July 1983.
Malcolm Batten

508 031 arrives at Wimbledon platform 5 on 19 April 1981, in the adjacent platform is the London Underground CO/CP stock farewell railtour. Peter Hoskins

side was left blank. The units were then renumbered to the 508/1 subclass by changing the fourth digit from a zero to a one. The units were then transferred to Kirkdale depot, where crew training was to take place. Due to the already in service 507 fleet, the introduction of the near identical 508s was quite straightforward, 508 142 and 143 worked in passenger service for the first time in March 1982 on the Southport line. The transfer of the remaining forty-one units did not begin in earnest until February 1983 as sufficient class 455s had been delivered and commissioned by the Southern Region at that time. Some units went straight to Birkenhead whilst others were stored at the Mollington Street Shed, a former loco depot in Birkenhead, until they could be processed. This location was also used to store redundant 503 units that the 508s were displacing. The last units moved north in the summer of 1984.

The bulk of the 508s were in service for the June 1984 timetable and they took over the bulk of the Wirral services between the loop line and Rock Ferry, New Brighton and West Kirby with a handful of 503 units hanging on until March 1985, after which time the 508s were the sole traction. The ambitions of both the Merseyside PTE and British Rail were for extensions to the third rail network on the Wirral. The extension from Rock Ferry to Hooton went live on 30 September 1985 and this resulted in an increase of services. Despite this, the provision of 508s and 507s for all the Merseyrail traffic was not over stretched, indeed there was a lot of spare capacity. Further extensions from Hooton to both Chester and Ellesmere Port were planned to come into effect in the 1990s. The former went live on 3 September 1993 and the latter on 29 May 1994. Despite this the fleet of forty-three 508 units together with thirty-two class 507 was able to meet the demands of the service with reduction in 6-car workings to just three cars in the off peak periods and by making the fleet interoperable and not limiting the 508s to the Wirral lines or the 507s to the Northern line. It was with this in mind that twelve class 508s were placed off lease as surplus in 1996 in the run up to privatisation of the network. The first private Merseyrail franchise was let to MTL Trust Holdings in January 1997. MTL was based in Liverpool and been set up as a bus and coach operator which was part owned by Merseyside PTE but had been bought out by management and staff in 1993. The 508 units, along with all passenger rolling stock previously owned by British Rail was sold to one of three rolling stock leasing companies (ROSCoS), Angel Trains got the 508s and the 507s with the 313s and 315s going to Eversholt. The 314 units were managed by Angel Trains but with involvement of the Strathclyde PTE.

The 508 fleet was put through a similar refurbishment between 2002 and 2005 to that given to the 507 units. This resulted in similar changes with new seating, new front end lighting and the fitting of CCTV. One of the distinctive features removed during this work was the remains of the original passenger door controls, both internally and externally. It was in this refurbished guise that all but fifteen of the fleet carried on their daily duties on either side of the River Mersey but for the fifteen units that left Merseyside there was other work elsewhere.

Rail privatisation had thrown up new options for the way services, and the rolling stock provided for them was managed. Train operating companies were no longer allocated a set of coaches and told to 'get on with it'; they had to lease their trains from the ROSCoS and therefore had the option to seek best value for money. The owners of the Southeastern franchise in Kent, Connex, wanted some cheap units to replace elderly slam door units on the branch lines and secondary routes they operated and they took a lease from Angel Trains on twelve units in 1997; these were 508 101/105/106/107/109/113/116/119/121/129/132 & 133. The units were transferred to Eastleigh Works where they underwent an overhaul and interior refreshment programme to the specifications of their new operator. This involved removing some of the seating to make more room for standing passengers and also bike and pram spaces. The seating that wasn't altered was still the original low backed plastic units they had been built with, albeit with replacement cushion covers. The whole fleet was painted in Connex Southeastern white and yellow livery and numbered to a new 508/2 sub-class with numbers applied from 508 201 up to 508 212 in the order of build, so the oldest unit became 201 and the newest was 212.

One other change was the re-instatement of the current collecting shoes on the cab end bogies with those on the trailing bogie of each driving car being removed. The units were allocated to Gillingham depot and after crew training entered service in August 1998 on the Sittingbourne to Sheerness-on-Sea, Strood to Paddock Wood/Tonbridge/Gatwick Airport and London Bridge to Tunbridge Wells services. Most services were operated by a single unit but some were diagrammed to a 6-car where platform lengths would allow. The 508/2s were never popular with passengers and they had reliability issues that blighted them. In 2006 the decision was taken to reduce the fleet to six units with just 203/205/207/208/210 & 211 kept in service. The remainder was stored or cannibalised for spare parts. The units were from then only used on the Sheerness-on-Sea and Maidstone services.

From 2005 Connex had been stripped of the franchise and it was being managed under the direct control of the Department for Transport as 'Operator of Last Resort'. A new livery had begun to be applied from 2005 to the 508s with the Connex yellow gone, replaced with a light grey stripe on the lower bodyside and a dark stripe around window level over the white body. The doors were painted yellow on the first version of the livery to make them contrast with the body but this was soon changed to pale blue on later repaints.

The units had C3/C4 exams carried out by Wabtec at Doncaster in June 2007. Time ran out for the 508s in Kent from 12 December 2008, after which the remaining six units were taken out of traffic with 2-car class 466 units taking over their remaining duties. The whole sub fleet were transported to Eastleigh works where they were to be scrapped. This was not the fate of all of them. Two driving vehicles, 64649 from 508 201 and 64712 from 508 209 ended up at Seacombe on the Wirral, where they were placed on concrete without rails and used at the emergency services training centre located there. 508 212 was reportedly taken to the fire training college at Moreton-in-Marsh; it is not known if any of the unit remains there.

The most novel upcycling of 508 coaches undertaken was by Arlington Fleet Services who operate the Eastleigh Works site. The driving cars from 508 207, numbered 64664 and 67707, were converted into translator coaches. This involved fitting conventional buffers and drawgear to the non-driving ends along with main reservoir and brake pipe air connections and LED tail light units, the driving ends kept their tightlock coupler gear and the internals of the coaches have been stripped out and a brake conversion unit fitted that translates the rises and falls in brake pipe pressure to Westcode signals that allow the brakes to be operated on units being towed by locomotives not fitted with Westcode brakes. This was a solution to an age old problem of transporting dead units around the network which had previously been done as unfitted goods trains at slow speeds. Indeed this wasn't the only such solution. Rail Operations Group developed a tightlock adaptor that can be fitted to locomotives in its fleet enabling them to couple to multiple units with the same coupler and an electrical connection was provided for a brake convertor on the locomotive to send Westcode brake signals to the multiple unit, thus enabling it to be hauled as a conventional trailing load. These locos were responsible for the movements of vast numbers of BREL '72 units to the scrapyards after their retirement and earned the locos the nickname of 'The Grim Reaper' among enthusiasts.

Three more off lease 508 units were taken up by the operator of the Euston to Watford services, Silverlink. These three were required to supplement the 313/1 fleet on the third rail route and were sent to Eastleigh Works for refurbishment and repainting into the company's purple, green and white livery with contrasting yellow doors. This work was undertaken in 2003 and also involved the units being re-wired so they were fully compatible with the 313/1 fleet for multiple working. The units did not have their shoe gear modified but had the trip cocks fitted as the line between Queens Park and Harrow and Wealdstone was fitted with this system. The units selected were 508 102/135 & 142 and upon refurbishment they were numbered into a 508/3 subclass as 508 301-303 in build order. They remained in traffic to the transition from Silverlink to TfL as operator of the route but were withdrawn early in the delivery of the 378 'Capitalstar' fleet and stored at Eastleigh Works. All three units were scrapped on site in 2013.

On Merseyside the replacement of the 508s was planned at the same time as the 507 fleet with the Stadler 777 fleet coming on line in the early 2020s. The 508s were to be withdrawn a few months earlier than the 507s and the 508 farewell rail tour ran on 29 October 2023 using units 508 139 + 141. The final 508 passenger working was undertaken in January 2024 by 508 104 on a service between Liverpool Central and New Brighton. The unit was then sent back to Birkenhead North depot and withdrawn. Over the coming months the remaining units made their final journey to Newport and a date with the cutters torch.

Before leaving the story of the 508s we have to go back to the beginnings and the story of the forty-three trailer cars removed from the original formations before they left the Southern Region. These vehicles were ordered and intended to be held back for inclusion in the second batch of replacement units, the project of which was classified as 510. The first batch had been the class 455/8 and these were not part of the BREL '72 family as they were built to a BR Mark III body profile on 20m frames and thus had a higher but flatter sided profile. The 455s had camshaft control but had a single motor coach in the middle of the formation and these re-used English Electric EE507 traction motors and DH 25 compressors reclaimed from withdrawn 4-SUB units. The second batch were to be built at York but it was decided that the three coaches would also be built to the same Mark III outline but with a revised cab front. The class 510 designation was dropped in favour of class 455/7 as the Southern Region had always numbered its EMUs in the 4XX series. This meant the 508 trailers that were to be inserted into those units were to be of a different outline. Coupling wise there wasn't a problem as the intermediate bar coupling was used on both types of stock. The removed trailers were stored at various locations, including Clapham Yard, Strawberry Hill, Wimbledon Park and Eastleigh Works. The first two 3-car 455/7 units were brought to the Southern Region in 1984 and delivered to Strawberry Hill depot where the ex-508 trailers were inserted. But subsequently it was decided to ship the trailers to York where they could be formed into the new units with all the rehabilitation work on the trailers carried out there. Some of the trailers had been in store for over a year. Forty-three 455/7 units were built, using up all of the ex-508 trailer cars.

One anomaly of these cars that persists to this day is their ability to confuse passengers when opening the doors. 455 cars require only a gentle tap on the open button for the doors to slide open but the 508 cars require the button to be pressed in for just over a second or they don't move. Many is the time I have sat in a 508 trailer and heard short bursts of air and a passenger stabbing at the button to find the doors not opening, usually cured by a shout of 'hold the button in'.

The whole 455 fleet was refurbished in the early to

508 TS vehicles removed from four car sets that had been sent north seen stored at Strawberry Hill. 15 February 1983. Colin Marsden

mid-2000s with new interior layout, 2 + 2 high backed seating and guards door controls added to the carriage interiors as South West Trains retained guards on their metro services and encouraged them to patrol the train and enabled them to work the doors from different coaches as they did so. The 508 coaches required additional thought for this programme due to their very different dimensions but the team at Eastleigh Works made it all happen and the fleet successfully went through the programme of works on time. At the time of writing, the ex-508 trailers are now the only way you can ride in a BREL '72 coach on the main line as the bulk of them remain in service. The whole 455 fleet was due to be replaced by class 701 units in the early 2020s but that plan has met with considerable delays and it is expected that the final replacement may not be completed until 2026.

Before the Class 508s were transferred to the Mersey electric system, the TS coaches were removed and stored for later installation in the Class 455/7 sets. TS cars 71567 and 71568 from sets 508042 and 508043, the first two 508s thus treated are seen inside the carriage and wagon shed at Clapham Junction on 18 August 1982. These coaches were later fitted into 455/7 sets 455713 and 455720. Colin Marsden

The penultimate station on the Shepperton branch is Upper Haliford, a station opened in wartime on 1 May 1944 to provide access to the Windmill Road industrial site, where parts of bombs were manufactured for the war effort. The station was very basic with concrete platforms, this remained until summer 2021 when a rebuild of the station saw its closure for several months. On 11 June 1981, set No. 508 036 pulls into the station with a Waterloo to Shepperton service. On the left is the M3 motorway. Colin Marsden

On 11 March 1981, Class 508 No. 508 024 approaches Richmond with a Waterloo (Windsor) to Waterloo (Main) via Kingston service. In the background is the Southern designed Richmond signal box, with a collection of old buses parked up in the former goods yard. Colin Marsden

Class 508s Nos. 508 005 and 508 013 depart from Ashsted station, between Epsom and Leatherhead, on 6 June 1981 with an all-stations service from Waterloo to Effingham Junction via Epsom. Colin Marsden

508 018 leads an eight car working through Hampton Court Junction. The destination blind implies the formation is bound for Wimbledon Park. Colin Marsden

508 028 has been reduced to three coaches and crudely renumbered to 508 128. It is seen here parked in one of the up bay platforms at Twickenham awaiting a tow to Merseyside. Peter Hoskins

Newly transferred 508 010 and the unit it would replace, class 503 M29288M at Mollington Street shed on Thursday 10 November 1984. Kev Smith

In service and renumbered 508 113 at Bebington, 6 September 1989. Malcolm Batten

508 136 was still wearing its BR blue and grey as late as 1996, seen here at Southport between duties. Author

Another unit late for repainting was 508 137 which is seen here at Southport on the rear of a service about to depart to Hunt's Cross. Author

508 126 at Hooton with the route set for Ellesmere Port. The unit is wearing the Regional Railways version of the Merseyrail livery. Author

508 102 at Chester, this unit had the lowest passenger miles of the fleet. On the Southern Region it had been held back for WSP trials and only released to passenger traffic for just over 18 months. The unit went off lease from Mersey Rail in 1997 and then did just over five years' service with Silverlink. For a class that existed for just over forty-four years, that wasn't a very good return. Author

Plans to keep the 508s on the Wirral lines were clearly not in place when this picture was taken of 508 123 + 122 on Northern Line duties at Southport in 1996. Author

508 129 was taken off lease in 1996 and would eventually go to Southeastern. Car M64720 was dumped at Southport with its batteries stripped out. Author

508 110 at Hooton before the electrification to Chester and Ellesmere Port, 9 July 1993.
Malcolm Batten

The old and the 'not so old'. 4-CIG unit 1811, on the left with the 12.00 Maidstone West to London Bridge, whilst 508 204 on the right with the 12.04 Maidstone West to Strood. Pictured at Maidstone West, Thursday 30 May 2002.
Colin Whitbread

508 212 at South Croydon wearing the white and yellow Connex South Eastern livery, 26 March 1999.
Malcolm Batten

508 202 arrive at Sheerness on Sea, for the launch of 508/2 sub-class by Connex South Eastern, 3 August 1998.
Colin Marsden

The rural nature of the line between Paddock Wood and Maidstone West is evident in this view of 508 205 working a Strood- Paddock Wood service over Swaithland Crossing. Tuesday 31 January 2006. Colin Whitbread

508 201 rounds the curve at Paddock wood having just departed with the 17.51 Paddock Wood to Strood service. Tuesday 20 September 2005. Colin Whitbread

508 208 approaching Redhill wearing the first version of the new South Eastern livery with the yellow doors, 6 September 2006. Malcolm Batten

In the second version of Southeastern livery with pale blue doors as introduced by new franchise operator 'Govia' 508 205 stands at Maidstone West with the 21.01 Paddock Wood-Strood (2T77), Monday 10 December 2007.
Colin Whitbread

508 203 has an early start at Strood, pictured here on the turnaround to work back to Gillingham having just arrived with the 04.45 ECS from Tonbridge (5Z51), Friday 28 September 2007.
Colin Whitbread

508 302 at Willesden Junction low level platforms on 12 July 2006 departing with a service to Watford Junction. The Silverlink livery made these blend in with the 313/1 fleet so only crews and enthusiasts could tell the difference. Colin Marsden

508 303 on 12 July 2006 arriving at Willesden Junction low level in Silverlink livery with a Watford Junction to Euston service. Colin Marsden

508 114 at Liverpool Central on the 'Loop' line. The single bore tunnel runs in a clockwise direction to keep trains to and from the Wirral circulating under the city centre. Author

***Above left*: With only** a few weeks left in service 508 131 calls at Port Sunlight with a service bound for the city, 26 October 2023. Author

***Above right*: The refurbished** interior of a 508 coach. Author

***Right*: The passenger** information display says this is the 14.42 service to West Kirby. The number on the front says the unit is 508 103 and anyone who knows the location doesn't need to look at the reflection in the windows to know this is James Street; the glazed tiles on the unused platform are a giveaway. 26 October 2023. Author

***Far left*: The ex-508** trailers were not inserted into the 455/7 units in build order and a fairly random approach appears to have been taken. This is 71546 which came from unit 508 021 but went into unit 455 712, seen here at Waterloo in South West Trains livery, 2 June 2021. Author

***Left*: The interior** of a 508 car in a 455/7 unit after the refurbishment undertaken for South West Trains. Author

Car 71552 which was originally part of 508 027 but now formed in 455 732. In the sunshine at Staines the contrast in outlines between the 508 car and the Mk. III driving car can be appreciated. Author

The driving coaches from 508 207 live on as translator barrier wagons. Seen here at Bexley on 11 November 2023 64664, now named Liwet, is the conversion between a class 66 and a class 465/9 unit. Richard Pickering

Coupling Conversion is also needed at the rear of the train and the other vehicle, 64707, now named Labezerin, is doing the honours. LED tail light clusters had been built into the body and the addition of buffers, draw hook and air pipes is evident. The vehicles retain the B1X bogies. Richard Pickering

Chapter 8

THE CLASS 315

The final fleet of units built as part of the BREL '72 family were the 4-car 315s, which, like the 507s and 314s, never strayed far from their original intended patch. These were also the largest single fleet of the family in terms of vehicles constructed that comprised the fleet. and being supplied by AC overhead wires at 25000V they were a direct follow on from the 314 units, being designed to the same specification from that 1975 document. In that document the 315s were envisaged as having two motored vehicles at one end, the driving motor and the pantograph motor car with a non-driving trailer and driving trailer making up the set. The units were going to be a 4-car version of the 314, achieved just by inserting an extra non driving trailer car. Between 1975 and 1979 the specification was obviously re-visited, as it was for the 314, with changes made for both types, there were also some regional specifications for the 315 that also appeared on the completed unit.

The lines they were to operate on were not newly electrified, indeed the Great Eastern suburban route had seen its first overhead electrification opened on 26 September 1949 when the line from Liverpool Street to Shenfield went live. This had been on an older 1500V DC system. It was extended to Chelmsford and Southend Victoria in 1956 but by this time attitudes to main line overhead electrification had changed with British Railways now keen to adopt the continental system using higher voltage AC wires which required considerably less lineside infrastructure than the DC system. What followed was a programme of conversion of both the electrification and the trains that ran on it from 1500V DC to, initially 6250V AC with new sections of electrification to Clacton and Chelmsford being installed at the new standard of 25000V AC. Additional suburban routes on the other side of Liverpool Street station, known as the West Anglia or Lea Valley lines were also electrified in sections at 25000V AC during the early 1960s with the wires reaching Chingford and Enfield Town, eventually reaching Broxbourne. Over the following decades both systems have now been fully electrified out as far as Cambridge and Norwich. The anomaly of the lower voltage 6250V AC system persisted for several decades and when the original DC stock was converted to operate from AC supply it had to be able to do so over the full range from the lower voltage right up to 25000V. The same applied to all the subsequent new stock built for the route and the 315s would also need to include an automatic feature that allowed them to operate from both supply pressures. Much like the lines around Liverpool that received the 507 and 508 units, the Great Eastern lines were already host to sliding door EMUs built to London Underground practice, the original 306 units that operated to Shenfield were built by Metro-Cammell and Birmingham Railway Carriage and Wagon Company and were 3-car units, these were built as 1500V DC supplied and proved to be excellent people movers for the busy services. Supplementing them were a fleet of British Railways built slam door units that became known as the 307s that, like the 306 units, had to be converted to operate from AC overhead wires.

Construction of the class 315 units was carried out at York Works from 1980 using the existing BREL '72 production line. The bodyshells and integral steel under frames were identical to the previous builds as were the internal fitting out of driving cabs, driving end lobby and passenger saloons. The bodies had the usual two pairs of passenger air operated doors on each side with a single leaf crew door to each lobby. The emergency escape door was on the cab front between the windows. Like the 508 units, the 315s were fitted with individual door open and close rubber buttons on the inside with door open buttons on either side of each pair of passenger doors on the outside of the body. The lighting, public address and heating and ventilation units were as per previous builds along with the standard plastic seating units with low backed seats and detachable cushions. In a change to the original specification, four traction motors were fitted to the driving cars, one on each axle with each driving car also having a CM38B compressor, along with the associated main air reservoir tanks. This type of compressor was different from other members of the family. These compressors were an older design and ran at 110V DC. They provided a degree of continuity with the equipment fitted to older units in the region. The compressors supplied the air for the doors, suspension, brakes and extra features such as the warning horn and window wipers. The transformer and rectifier set was fitted to one of the trailer cars which also housed the Stone Faiveley AMBR Mk. 1 pantograph on the roof and a 110V battery pack was fitted to the underframe of the transformer trailer car. That car also had a battery charger that took a feed tapped off the output from the transformer rectifier and was stepped down to 110V DC to keep the batteries in a state of constant charge. The feed also supplied all of the train control circuits and the lighting which was split into three sections on each coach, two main lighting circuits and an emergency lighting circuit. Each had its own inverter which fed the fluorescent tubes but in the event of the overhead AC supply to the pantograph failing, only the main lights would go out, with the emergency lights receiving a supply from the batteries to maintain a low level of lighting during the supply problem. The batteries also supplied control systems and the incandescent lighting in the cab, lobby and the train's head, marker and red tail lights. This system did away with the need to fit a motor alternator set to the units.

The other trailer car had no extra equipment fitted and was the lightest vehicle in the formation at 25.5 tons, the driving motor cars weighed in at 35 tons with the pantograph trailer slightly less at 32 tons. A mix of Brush TM61-53 and GEC G310AZ traction motors were fitted to the units. These were again rated at 110hp each and were fully interchangeable. The units, like all classes in the BREL '72 family, had a maximum design speed of 75mph, but due to the nature of the classes working suburban routes with frequent stops the opportunities to go that fast were very limited. Wheel slide/slip protection (WSP) equipment was fitted in the form of the BR Mark II system which, like the 508s, was to be problematic. The other standard features found on other classes such as the air suspension with self-levelling valves for heavier loading period and the three step Westcode brakes were also found on the 315s but they were not fitted with any form of rheostatic braking, relying on the friction disk brakes only as per the 314 units. Above the driver's window was a roller blind for the destination whilst above the non-driving side cab window were four individual roller blinds for displaying the train reporting number. This second feature didn't last long before it was removed. A 4-car unit had seating for 318 passengers in as-built condition and the specification was that up to three units could run in multiple, making a 12-car train if needed but in reality the platforms were mostly unable to accept a train that long on the routes they were to work.

Of the sixty-one units built it was envisioned that forty-one of them would be provided for the Liverpool Street to Shenfield route with the remaining twenty allocated to the Lea Valley West Anglia lines. The units were all painted in the same corporate blue and grey with full yellow end and black cab front window surrounds and numbered 315 801 to 315 861. Deliveries commenced to Ilford depot in the summer of 1980 where the units were to be commissioned and early crew training was undertaken. Like other stock, the delivery runs required the use of coupling translator wagons due to the incompatibility of the tightlock couplings and had to be run at low speed due to the lack of train brakes. The first batch of units were commissioned in time for some to enter passenger service from December 1980 but it would not be until the late summer of 1981 that the whole fleet was in traffic on both the Shenfield and Lea Valley routes. Units rarely strayed from their designated patch. One unit was sent to Southend Central to be demonstrated, but the Fenchurch Street to Tilbury and Southend lines would have to wait several more years for anything as modern as a 315 to make an appearance on a regular basis. The units settled into their regular mundane duties, ferrying thousands of commuters each day to and from Liverpool Street. Very little changed for them and the units were considered reliable, but there were concerns amongst crews over the WSP equipment which turned into an industrial dispute in the late 1980s. Within a few years of their introduction, the upgrades to the overhead electrification out of Liverpool Street eliminated the last sections of the old 6250V AC with all lines now energised at 25000V. The units gained Network SouthEast livery along with every other unit in that part of the country, the first example of the livery did away with the black front window surrounds and the full yellow end looked very odd, but the black was quickly re-instated on subsequent repaints. The fleet gained additional work to Southend Victoria on Saturdays when there was less demand for units on the Shenfield route, but as a whole they rarely strayed from their normal stomping grounds. The lack of toilets made them unsuitable for longer runs and they were designed and utilised as suburban stock. From the start of the 1990s, driver only operation was introduced on the routes with the units fitted with driver door control and cab radios with banks of monitors at stopping points on the platforms so the driver could observe passengers boarding and alighting and know when it was safe to close the doors.

Rail privatisation came in the late 1990s with the whole 315 fleet passing into the ownership of Eversholt Rail Group who leased them to the respective operators. The lines out of Liverpool Street were divided into two distinct franchises along historic boundaries with the Great Eastern Franchise, let to First Group, taking the lines to Norwich, including the Shenfield route and thus forty-three 315 units with the Lea Valley lines coming under the West Anglia and Great Northern franchise, initially let to PRISM Rail but later National Express, who got the remaining eighteen units. New liveries followed and units on the Great Eastern started appearing at different locations with the odd example making it as far as Ipswich when other stock wasn't available. Other units turned up at Clacton, Colchester and a West Anglia set made it as far as Cambridge on at least one occasion. From April 2004 both the Great Eastern and West Anglia lines were combined under one Greater Anglia Franchise which was let to National Express. This allowed for the 315 fleet to be managed as a single entity and in 2008 all sixty-one units were put through a half-life rebuild at a cost of £60 million. The work was undertaken by Bombardier at Ilford and was quite comprehensive. The air-operated passenger doors were changed to electric motor operation, all the passenger windows were replaced with new units that looked similar but did away with the leaking seals and water traps, the interior got new seat covering, albeit on the original half back plastic units and CCTV was fitted.

Underneath the train, the problematic Mark II WSP equipment was removed in favour of a new Westinghouse system. This was a marked improvement and resulted in considerably fewer wheel flats and inspired greater confidence amongst the drivers. The units were by now all painted in the ONE livery but the franchise was rebranded at the time of the refresh to become National Express East Anglia. The franchise was again re-let in February 2012 to Abellio which prompted another change in livery for the 315 fleet. The new operators spent further on upgrades to the fleet with the installation of LED lighting, wheelchair spaces and new passenger information displays and automated announcements. The units also started appearing on the Romford to Upminster branch line, which was a short branch line requiring only a single 4-car set to operate it. A further change in operator occurred on 31 May 2015 when the Lea Valley lines from Liverpool Street to Enfield Town, Cheshunt and Chingford, along with the Romford to Upminster line were transferred to TfL, run directly by the Greater London Assembly, this resulted in twenty units being transferred to the London Overground fleet who re-liveried them into their colours over the next few months. The remaining forty one sets were passed to MTR Elizabeth Line who took over the running of the Liverpool Street to Shenfield route in preparation for that line becoming a part of the 'Crossrail' project that would see new trains running in tunnels under London on to Heathrow and eventually Reading, but the 315s would never work in the tunnels, remaining on the Liverpool Street to Shenfield section. These units were painted in a simpler white livery with blue lower bodyside stripe.

Both operators made clear their desire to replace the 315s from the outset. MTR were taking delivery of new class 345 units for the full Crossrail introduction and London Overground had ordered 4-car 710 units for their services, both fleets were to be built at Derby by Bombardier. The rundown of the 315 fleet began in 2019 with London Overground being the first to introduce their replacements. A final day was run for a pair of 315s on 20 October 2020 on timetabled services which visited Enfield Town and ended up at Chingford with 315 802 and 807 doing the honours. TfL even had special pens and badges made marking the end of the 315s which were given out to passengers and a DJ and free tea and coffee was supplied to meet the final train at Chingford. The Elizabeth Line units held on a few years longer with gradual introduction of 7-car 345s eroding the fleet and this was further compounded when the platforms at Liverpool Street were rebuilt to handle a full length nine car 345 service. The final working occurred on 9 December 2022 with the 18:04 Liverpool Street to Gidea Park. After that all the units bar two made the journey to South Wales for scrap, being quickly broken up. 315 853 was sent to Booth's scrapyard in Rotherham where the intention was to allow recovery of parts for the restoration of 313 201 by the National Collection, that project never happened but 853 did yield parts for other BREL '72 preservation projects before being finally broken up in 2024. 315 856 did not go for scrap as it was secured for preservation and that story will be told elsewhere. A service life of 42 years was considered a decent return on the whole class and they had become quite popular with crews and local enthusiasts. Before the end of their service a farewell railtour was run by the Branch Line Society on 26 November 2022 and was well patronised.

In the original BR blue and grey livery, 315 805 enters Manor Park on a morning train all stations to Gidea Park. 26 April 1985. Malcolm Batten

315 810 at Cambridge Heath, 16 March 1987. While the train is in BR blue and grey, NSE branding adorns the station. The platforms here and at London Fields are only on two of the four tracks and only Enfield and Cheshunt line services stop here. For many years these stations were only served during weekday peak periods, with regular daytime services not restarting until 1998, and evening and Saturday services from 2001. Malcolm Batten

The first built unit 315 801 at wearing Network SouthEast livery at Upminster, 17 August 1989. Malcolm Batten

Network SouthEast was not just about the livery of the trains, it was about creating a brand and as such the station were to match. This view of 315 860 at Hertford East shows they got it right, 9 April 1994.
Malcolm Batten

315 812 at Manor Park, 21 July 1988.
Malcolm Batten

315 825 and 859 pass at Hackney Downs, 7 August 1988.
Malcolm Batten

A view of not just 315 835, but of the western side of Liverpool Street station before it was extensively rebuilt. Of interest is the nearly new 321 unit and the Mark 1 buffet car in a loco hauled set. 14 October 1990.
Malcolm Batten

First Great Eastern livery was the first privatisation colour scheme for the 315s, worn here by 315 805 at Manor Park on fast line due to engineering work, 16 August 1998. Malcolm Batten

On shuttle duty 315 840 is seen at Upminster working back and forth to Romford, 26 August 2000. Malcolm Batten

315 801 at Southminster on what appears to be a quiet period, 4 August 2001. Malcolm Batten

Wearing the plain white livery of the West Anglia and Great Northern franchise 315 845 is pictured at Stratford, 17 June 1999. Malcolm Batten

315 844 at Hackney Downs, 14 June 2002.
Malcolm Batten

No, that isn't graffiti, it was a script graphic added to the plain white WAGN livery to promote the Travelcard on 315 845, pictured at Hackney Downs, 13 September 2000.
Malcolm Batten

WAGN switched to a blue livery with white doors as seen here on 315860 at Hackney Downs, 14 June 2002. Malcolm Batten

315 804 in the blue livery with white doors but with Great Eastern branding, seen at Manor Park. This unit has received the modified head and marker/taillight clusters that were fitted to a number of class members during refurbishment, 3 June 2004. Malcolm Batten

Another unit painted in a livery to promote the London 2012 Olympic Games bid was 315812 passing Pudding Mill Lane, 31 May 2005.
Malcolm Batten

The colourful National Express 'One' livery adorns 315 813, seen here passing Pudding Mill Lane, 31 May 2005.
Malcolm Batten

The stock controllers must have been short of units on 21 October 2006 as 315 848 is at Shenfield forming a service back to Liverpool Street solo, quite rare for these services to be just four coaches. Malcolm Batten

On 11 May 2008 315 812 stops on the fast line platform at Manor Park with a train from Liverpool Street to Gidea Park. A blue livery is carried but devoid of any branding, the ONE brand having been dropped in February. Malcolm Batten

In de-branded ONE livery 315 806 pictured at Manor Park, 11 May 2008. Malcolm Batten

315 826 at Manor Park (fast line). Light blue livery with white band and National Express name. 15 September 2008. Malcolm Batten

In February 2012, Abellio Greater Anglia took over the franchise. 315 824 is seen at Goodmayes is in their livery on 25 April 2015 but without any ownership branding as TfL would take over the service from 31 May. Malcolm Batten

315 854 at Manor Park in Abellio Greater Anglia white with red doors but now with the TfL roundel added to the bodysides to signify that they have taken over the operation of the route. Malcolm Batten

Since 31 May 2015 the services to Chingford, Enfield and Cheshunt via Seven Sisters were operated as part of London Overground. 315 815 entering Walthamstow Central in 2015 shows the livery adopted for the units that served these routes.
Malcolm Batten

315 803 passes another of the class at Bethnal Green in 2016.
Malcolm Batten

315 815 at Enfield Town 06 October 2020. Author

The afternoon of 20 October 2020 witnessed the last London Overground service on the Lea Valley lines operated by a 315. 315 802 is seen here at Liverpool Street being readied for the final passenger run to Chingford. Author

The last 315 service to arrive at Chingford had 315 807 on the back. Despite the need for social distancing due to the COVID 19 pandemic London Overground put on a bit of an event to see the 315s were given a send off. Author

Manor Park, June 2015 and 315 850 has received the simple MTR livery with roundel. Malcolm Batten

The interior of a 315 during its later life with MTR Elizabeth Line. The layout has been changed nearest the camera but the rest of the car is very much as it always has been except the colour scheme. Author

***Above left*: Unlike many** other BREL '72 fleets the 315s never lost the low backed plastic seating units with detachable cushions they were built with. The moquette is a TfL one and the red infused seat is designated as a priority see for those who need to sit more than others. Author

***Above right*: 315 844** at Liverpool Street getting ready for another run to Shenfield 20 September 2021. Author

***Right*: Two British** Rail built classes side by side and both nearing the end of their working lives, 315 838 and 321 301 at Liverpool Street 08 June 2021. Author

Journeys end for the 315s for many decades, 315 853 at Shenfield 20 September 2021.
Author

In the run up to Remembrance Sunday TfL underground, overground and tram stock wear poppy vinyls as a mark of respect. 315 847 was still wearing its poppy as late as 24 November 2022, seen here at Liverpool Street.
Author

The soon to be preserved 315 856 pictured at Gidea Park on the penultimate day of 315 operations, having just arrived with an evening peak extra from Liverpool Street which were the last duties the class were allocated in their final weeks, 8 December 2022. Author

Class 37 diesel electric locomotive 37 884, officially named *Cepheus* but to many enthusiasts it is known as 'The Grim Reaper' due to its involvement with towing withdrawn units away to scrap yards. Author

Close up of the tightlock coupling adaptor fitted to 37 884, shown here in the raised position the adaptor can be lowered to expose the conventional draw hook and allow the locomotive to couple to buffered stock. Author

Chapter 9

EPILOGUE

The story cannot be completed without making a mention here of the sixth class member in the family, the one that never made it beyond the drawing board; the class 316, an EMU intended for a new link line running in a tunnel under Manchester between Manchester Victoria and Manchester Piccadilly stations, with the line from Bury feeding it from one side whilst the one from Hazel Grove and Buxton would link to the other. The lines involved would all have been electrified at 25000V AC. The proposal was for a fleet of new class 316 units based on the work done on the PEP prototypes and 920 001 to be built to serve it. Despite this, the tenders for their construction were never issued. A lot of preparatory work and feasibility studies were carried out by both British Rail and the Greater Manchester Passenger Transport Executive in 1975 but the project was never authorised and had been officially cancelled by 1977, thus the Class 316 never happened as a member of the BREL '72 family, though the class number was re-used in later years for an unrelated unit. The lines under consideration eventually got rebuilt as part of the Manchester Metrolink tram network with a surface tram line between Manchester's Victoria and Piccadilly stations.

As the bulk of the units have now completed their last duties and have been consigned to history we can evaluate the story of the BREL '72 family in full and can only regard it as a successful one. Whilst the units performed everyday mundane work and never had the glamour or excitement of high speed crack express trains, their service impacted the lives of millions of people. Those people undertook the journeys on the units because they needed to; their livelihoods depended on being able to get to work and their family lives depended on being able to get home again. Without doubt, as is the case with any public transport infrastructure, there were days when it didn't go quite to plan, and unfortunately it tends to be those days that get remembered when people recall their time commuting and not the ones where the complexities of running an intense service went to the plan, which more often than not it did. These units also represented a time when British Rail had started to learn to live with the mistakes of its past and deliver trains and services that were what were expected of it for the age in which it was operating. The shock and awe of the Beeching period may well be one of the most significant and controversial periods in the history of the Britain's railway network but there is a degree of thinking that at that time things had to change and that change had to come. The railway that resulted from it went ahead with a new mindset, sense of purpose and vision and gave rise to not only the BREL '72 fleet but the Inter City 125 and modular freight traffic, driver-only operation, passenger focus groups and clock face timetables whilst bringing a railway that was still based upon Victorian infrastructure and equally outdated operating principles into the modern age. That transition took decades to achieve, was it all good? Not at all, but it also wasn't a disaster. Was it needed? Absolutely. Many people may disagree and indeed the resistance to change took years to overcome and shape the railway network we have today which is still evolving of course.

It is also worth noting that never again would British Rail build a multiple unit that had slam doors or no provision for standing passengers, the Westcode and rheostatic brakes became the standard for all EMUs that followed the BREL '72 fleet and that will be their legacy; they were truly ground breaking and set the new bar for British Rail. This is not just the story of eleven prototype and 755 production vehicles that were built to do a job, it is a record of a significant moment of change in the history of Britain's railway network.

Appendix 1

THE PRESERVED UNITS

My involvement with the idea of 313 preservation began during that online meeting organised by the RHDAB as mentioned in my introduction. I was passionate about the need to represent the BREL '72 fleet in the National Collection and the paper I produced led to some high level discussions, which I was not part of but was kept informed on, regarding 313 201 and the possibility of reverting it back as near as possible to its original specification. Beacon Rail had agreed the unit should be preserved and Eversholt Rail Group were willing to help out by making seats and pantograph equipment available from a 315 unit. The unit even appeared on the National Railway Museum website as a hoped-for future acquisition. It appeared to all be going so well. The RHDAB had placed a designation on 313 201 which meant it had to be offered for preservation. Then it started to go wrong. I was not privy to the decisions made elsewhere so will only tell the parts I know. The Science Museum Group, who have overall control of not only the Science Museum but several other national institutions, including the National Railway Museum, were not convinced. This was the period when the country was living with the COVID 19 pandemic and museums were shut, the future looked very uncertain and thus budgets were kept on a tight leash. Whatever decisions were made resulted in the National Railway Museum rejecting the idea of reverting 313 201 back to near original condition, which kind of flew in the face of the arguments made why it should be included in the National Collection. Some discussions were held and the designation was lifted from 313 201 and placed upon 313 121 which was with Network Rail and still had both AC and DC capability. It was missing sections of its original interior and could not boast to have been the first unit built in the BREL '72 family, but it did make for a suitable example of the class and the story they told. Then came the news that the National Collection had no budget to preserve any class 313 so even 313 121 was being rejected. This was a major blow and Mike Lamport and I had a few discussions about what options there were for an alternative home for the designated 313. What followed next though was the start of a chain of units entering preservation so I will look at them in the order they happened.

313 121

Having been involved in EMU preservation for several decades I got to know a few people and also got invited to partake in a few group discussions, both in the real world and online. The discussion of what to do with the class 314 hydrogen unit when its test programme was completed was one such debate, which happened on WhatsApp of all places. The chat involved a few key players with inside knowledge of the project and the railway preservation scene in Scotland, not something I know much about. I have to confess that the idea of 314 preservation was something that had completely passed me by and I was a participant in the discussions but not the most informed one.

From the discussions came the news that the unit was not being released from the Bo'ness and Kinneil Railway anytime soon, but that one site, the Fife Heritage Railway at Leven, would be open to taking the whole set if it were to become available. A few months after this, the issue with 313 121 and the National Collection came

313 121 in the yard at the Fife Heritage Railway at Leven. Khai Slater

to pass and I remember having a light bulb moment. Would the railway at Leven take a 313 instead of a 314? I contacted Khai Slater, a Fife Heritage Railway volunteer who had been involved in the WhatsApp discussion on the 314 and floated the 313 idea past him. He was keen but would need to convince the rest of the railway's board. The reply came back that yes, they were very interested but the whole project had to be cost effective for it to go ahead. My next step was to speak with both Mike Lamport and the disposals people at Network Rail who were desperate to find a home for 313 121. This was an online meeting and I was very happy to announce I had a taker for the unit but there was the issue of money that needed to be resolved. Needless to say, the unit was donated and it was just the transport costs that had to be covered. An arrangement was made that would see all three cars of 313 121 transported from store and delivered to Leven. The move took three days to achieve and was completed by 21 August 2023 with a convoy of three lorries, each carrying a 313 vehicle travelling to Leven where the vehicles were unloaded and work could begin on reforming the unit. Supplied with 313 121 were coupling adaptors that enabled the unit to be shunted around the yard. The vehicles were subject to a vandalism attack which resulted in several broken windows but a crowdfunding campaign supported by social media star Francis Bourgeois raised some funds and the replacement of the windows has now been carried out. The volunteers at Leven are very pleased with their new acquisition and keep the batteries topped up with charge and the air system gets regular use. 313 121 has

The vehicles of 313 121 at the end of their long journey from Leicestershire arriving at Leven in convoy.
Steven Carty

Frosty sleepers and frozen windows. 313 121 getting used to its new life in Scotland. Khai Slater

generated extra interest in the Fife Heritage Railway, especially from younger members and the unit will be a prized fixture of their fleet going forward.

313 201

Having missed out in a place in the National Collection the future looked bleak for the first built of the 313 fleet. That was until late June 2023 when the unit was taken to Eastleigh Works along with the other eighteen of its Southern classmates upon their retirement with the expectation all would be broken up on site there. Peter Spokes, who trades as 400 Series Preservation Group and owns vehicles of VEP and CIG ancestry announced on the group Twitter and Facebook feeds that he was in discussions to take on 313 201 and keep it at Eastleigh in what can best be described as 'warm storage' as it would have access to live conductor rails from time to time and would also be able to be kept in operational condition. Peter appealed for supporters to

contribute a monthly fee towards the cost of the storage. In August it was announced that he had agreed terms and was now the owner of 313 201. Over the next eighteen months he organised a select number of driver experience days, whereby visitors could visit Eastleigh Works and take the controls of 313 201 along a length of electrified siding, making 313 201 the only privately owned EMU to officially run from the third rail in Britain in this century. These 'days', along with the supporters' club, have generated much needed revenue to keep the unit at Eastleigh but time is running out on that agreement and the unit is due to leave there to attend the Greatest Gathering at Derby Works in August 2025, after which the next long term home for 313 201 is yet to be confirmed.

315 856

A few years before the end of 315 operations with MTR and TfL, a group of enthusiasts had gathered together and formed the

313 201 berthed between duties at Brighton on 13 August 2021. Around the time that the preservation of this unit was considered assured. Author

The first vehicle of 315 856 unloaded at Cynheidre, the headquarters of the LMMR on 10 January 2023. Mark Thomas

315 Preservation Group with the intention of saving a complete 4-car unit. The idea gained traction via the group's active Facebook group and eventually merchandise was sold to raise funds. A formally constituted group was formed that people could join for a fee, a website was created and, importantly, serious discussions were held with the owners of the 315 fleet, Eversholt, over the details of such a sale to the group. What was missing was a home for the unit. Initially, an approach to store it at the Crewe Heritage Centre was provisionally arranged but this was never properly signed off and for reasons unknown the idea went no further. The group identified 315 820 as their first choice of unit and all publicity was centred around this. An agreement to locate the unit to the Llanelli and Mynydd Mawr Railway (LMMR) in South Wales was reached, which was a long way from 315 operating territory but as the only site that said yes to the group's approaches it was better than no home and therefore no 315 preservation. As the end drew near for 315 820, a snag occurred that meant that unit would not become available for preservation and would go for scrap instead. The group were offered their choice from the remaining operational sets and decided upon 315 856. Once withdrawn from traffic there was the issue of getting it from Ilford to South Wales which had to be achieved by taking the unit by rail to the

All four coaches of 315 856 pictured at Cynheidre on 19 August 2023. The vehicles are not coupled up due to the need to move them from time to time which saves on unbolting couplings. When the vehicles have a more permanent location within the site then they will be re-coupled. Author

Dean Forest Railway from where it could be moved by road to its new home. The first coach moved in appalling weather conditions during January 2023 and was not the easiest delivery. It was a few weeks later when the remaining three coaches were delivered in better weather. Everything appeared to be going well but one day a few months later the road haulier contacted the group to say that payment for the move was still outstanding. The management of the group were stunned to learn that not only had the invoices not been paid but the money they had raised over the last few years had disappeared. An investigation is still ongoing into this matter so I can comment no further at this time. What I can say is that two group officers used their own savings to settle the invoices but the group was now in disarray. Items of merchandise that had been ordered by supporters could not be delivered, memberships could not be taken, the group did not have access to its bank account and there was now no income and no money. The group has spent the last eighteen months trying to rebuild from the serious fraud it suffered. That work remains ongoing but 315 856 is still at the LMMR. The group was able to earn some money in 2024 when one car of the unit was transported back to the Dean Forest Railway to be hired for a filming contract. At the time of writing, a new management team and a new organisation is being set up to take the 315 preservation project forward.

507 001

With withdrawals of 508 and 507 units gathering pace on Merseyside, local enthusiast Robert Hampton decided to see what interest was out there in saving the original unit from that generation, 507 001, for preservation. Social media posts were made to promote the idea and Robert organised a formal meeting for all of those interested held in Liverpool on 19 November 2023. The meeting was well attended and a formal constitution for the 507 Preservation Society was agreed with a management committee put in place. Over the next few weeks, discussions were held with Angel Trains over the terms and conditions

507 001 posed in V Shop at Alstom Derby on 2 May 2025. Class 507 Preservation Society

under which 507 001 would be made available. Robert wrote to almost every heritage railway in England and Wales asking if they would have space to host the 507 unit. Only one replied that they would and that was the Tanat Valley Railway at Nantmawr in Shropshire. What was needed next was the money to get the unit transported to its new home. The group launched a crowdfunding page to raise £10 000 and the message was spread by social media. BBC local radio and even television picked up on this story and it gained a lot of attention and as a result the crowdfunder broke through its target and ended up raising £14,000 for the project. The news came just before the units were withdrawn from traffic that 507 001 was to be invited to Alstom's Derby Litchurch Lane Works for storage ahead of being an exhibit at the Greatest Gathering which would be held at the site in August 2025. 507 001 was delivered to Newport on 23 January 2025 and was then put on lorries and taken to Derby. Once at Derby the group has been allowed access to carry out renovation and inspection of their unit and it has been powered up on the work's DC equipped test track. The intention is still to take the unit to Nantmawr after the event in August.

Volunteers pose with 507 001 after a day working on the unit at Derby, 1 March 2025. Left to right Matthew Carville, Jake D'Arcy, Tom Camps, Shaun Henry and Jamie Connerty.
Class 507 Preservation Society

508 201 (vehicle 64649)

The 508s were looking as if they would miss out on preservation. Many people were hoping 'The Beatles' liveried set would find salvation but no credible plan ever emerged and all of the Merseyrail units went for scrap. Then, in a move that came out of the blue, Peter Spokes acquired one of the ex-Southeastern driving motor cars from the fire training centre at Seacombe on the Wirral. The vehicle was brought back to Kent in November 2024 and delivered to the East Kent Railway in Shepherdswell where 400 Series Preservation has a number of other vehicles stored. Peter announced that his intention was to rebuild the vehicle as a translator coach to allow 313 201 to be hauled on a heritage railway with the brakes being translated as they are on the Arlington Fleet ex 508 coaches and buffers, draw hooks and conventional air connections fitted to the non-driving end. To date Peter has carried out work on the tightlock coupling, reinstating the connection block and has got the wiring sorted in the driving cab and the saloon lights working. This is an ambitious project and if completed would open up the wider heritage movement to Westcode braked stock.

64649 from 508 201 seen immediately after delivery to the East Kent Railway at Shepherdswell. James Pickering

64649 seen on 17 November 2024, work has been undertaken to remove the worst of the graffiti and since this picture was taken further electrical work has been progressed.
Author

Appendix 2

VEHICLE TYPES AND NUMBERS

Class 445 4-PEP Units 4001 & 4002

Vehicle Type	Vehicle Number Range
Driving Motor Second Open	64301 – 64304 B type car
Motor Second Open	62426 – 62429 C type car

Class 446 2-PEP Unit 2001

Vehicle Type	Vehicle Number Range
Driving Motor Second Open	64300 A type car
Driving Motor Second Open	64305 B type car

Class 920 Unit 920 001

Vehicle Type	Vehicle Number Range
Driving Motor Second Open	975430 (formerly 64300)
Driving Motor Second Open	975432 (formerly 64305)
Pantograph Trailer Open	975431

Class 313 Unit 313 001 – 313 064

Vehicle Type	Vehicle Number Range
Driving Motor Second Open	62529 – 62592 (A end cars)
Pantograph Trailer Second Open	71213 – 71276
Battery Driving Motor Second Open	62593 – 62656 (B end cars)

Class 314 Unit 314 201 – 314 216

Vehicle Type	Vehicle Number Range
Driving Motor Second Open	64583 – 64613 (odd numbers only)
Pantograph Trailer Second Open	71450 – 71465
Driving Motor Second Open	64584 – 64614 (even numbers only)

Class 315 Unit 315 801 – 315 861

Vehicle Type	Vehicle Number Range
Driving Motor Second Open	64462 – 64582 (even numbers only)
Pantograph Trailer Second Open	71389 – 71449
Trailer Second Open	71281 – 71341
Driving Motor Second Open	64461 – 64581 (odd numbers only)

Class 507 Unit 507 001 – 508 033

Vehicle Type	Vehicle Number Range
Driving Motor Second Open	64405 – 64437 (A end cars)
Trailer Second Open	71342 – 71374
Battery Driving Motor Second Open	64367 – 64734 (B end cars)

Class 508 Unit 508 001 – 508 043

Vehicle Type	Vehicle Number Range
Driving Motor Second Open	64649 – 64691 (A end cars)
Trailer Second Open	71483 – 71525
Trailer Second Open	71526 – 71568 (reformed in 455/7 units)
Battery Driving Motor Second Open	64692 – 64399 (B end cars)

BIBLIOGRAPHY

British Rail (Southern), Chief Operating Manager, 1972 Type, High Density PEP Stock, Drivers Handout, 1971

British Rail (Southern), Chief Operating Manager, Class 508 EMUs, Drivers Guide to Faults & Failures, 1979

British Railways Board, CM&EE Department, Outline Specification For Class 314 and Class 315 Electric Multiple Units, 1975

Cooper B. K., *Electric Trains in Britain*, Ian Allan Ltd, 1979

GEC Traction, General Description, Protective Devices & Fault Indicator Lights, 1985

Howat, Colin J, *Class 314 EMUs in Scotland*, Amberley Publishing, 2024

Marsden, Colin J, *Southern Electric Multiple Units 1948-1983*, Ian Allan Ltd, 1983

Vickers, R. L, *DC Electric Trains & Locomotives in the British Isles*, David & Charles, 1986

www.bloodandcustard.com/BR-4PEP.html, John Atkinson/C. Watts

history pages at www.scot-rail.co.uk, (various contributors)

Scottish Trains Website, www.scottishtrains.zenfolio.com

Smilie, Liam, Glasgow Central Floods, Glasgow World Website.

INDEX

Batteries 16, 17, 40, 70, 78, 90, 94, 120, 145
Beeching, Dr. Richard 9
Brakes 17, 18, 23, 35, 40, 70, 78, 79, 93-96, 99, 120, 142
British Rail Engineering Limited (BREL) 10, 12, 13, 26, 39, 70, 78

Collisions;
  Hyndland Junction 79
  Kirkby 71
  Kirkdale 71
  Newton 80
Compressor 17, 35, 40, 70, 78, 79, 93, 94, 99, 120
Couplings 13, 14, 23, 29, 40, 79, 94, 100, 120, 141

Door Operation 11, 12, 14, 40, 42, 71, 78, 79, 94, 95, 100, 120, 121

Glasgow Floods 80

Local Government Act 70

Manchester Metrolink 142
Match Wagon 23, 27, 29, 30, 99, 118
Modernisation Plan 8-10, 12, 39
Motor Alternator 15-18, 35, 40, 70, 78, 94, 120

Passenger Transport Authorities 9, 70, 79, 142

Railway Technical Centre 10, 12, 13, 17, 26, 29, 32, 34-38, 66
Railtours 46, 47, 62, 65, 77, 82, 97, 122
Royal Visits 71, 79

Suspension 17, 18, 25, 40, 120

Traction Interlock 95
Traction Motors 16, 18, 40, 78, 90, 93, 99, 120
Transport Act 9, 70

Ventilation 15, 26, 39, 40, 79, 94, 120

Wheel Slip/Slide Protection (WSP) 93-96, 120, 121